PEAK DIS

TEASHOP
WALKS

Charles Wildgoose

COUNTRYSIDE BOOKS
NEWBURY BERKSHIRE

COUNTRYSIDE BOOKS
3 Catherine Road
Newbury, Berkshire

**To view our complete range of books,
please visit us at
www.countrysidebooks.co.uk**

ISBN 978 1 85306 775 4

Designed by Graham Whiteman
Cover illustration by Colin Doggett
Maps and photographs by the author

Produced through The Letterworks Ltd., Reading
Typeset by KT Designs, St Helens
Printed by The Holywell Press, Oxford

Contents

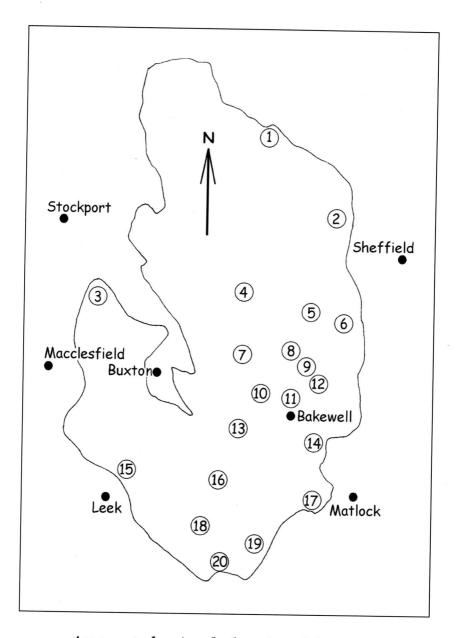

Area map showing the location of the walks

Acknowledgements

These walks were devised by my father and tested by him and as ever, with Balkees. They were assisted in the original edition by the following group of testers: Alex Pryor and Sharon Price; Chris, Julia and Charlotte Gale; Louis McMeeken, Christine and Josie the collie; Hilary and Brian Hoon; Paul Hopkins; Angela Waite and Anne Wiles; myself – Jamie Wildgoose – and Hannah Cooper; Ron and Elizabeth Haydock; Adrian Partridge; Daniel Bayfield, Lee Hobson and Lesley Stone; Ruth Rhodes and Amanda Wardman.

Later, for the 2010 update, testing was handled by Ruth, Graham and Tom Rhodes (and Mattie) as well as their friend Anna.

Finally, for this new 2017 update, Ruth and Graham Rhodes, along with Balkees, joined Angela Bush, myself, and – with very special thanks – Sophie Bush.

Introduction

It is over twenty years now since my late father, Charles Wildgoose, was asked to write his first volume for Countryside Books. He took to it like any walker takes to the hills on a bright Sunday morning – with the utmost enthusiasm. But how could he not? Having lived his whole life in Derbyshire, he knew every road and path, every view and hedgerow, and it was his pleasure to bring his wide ranging local knowledge to an even wider audience.

In this, the first of his books to be fully revised and updated since his death in 2013, Dad turns his attention to the Peak District – in it he takes us through beautiful old woods and around scenic reservoirs. You will pass through a landscape that has been visited by kings (Peveril Castle), frequented by wallabies (The Roaches), worked by Quakers (Monyash) and menaced by highwaymen (Black Harry Gate) … and you can throw in Little John and Robin Hood for good measure.

This book isn't just about exploring the Peak District's varied scenery though. It's also about exploring teashops – and what an interesting collection they are. There's one in a garden centre, another in a renovated coach house, a third in a converted joinery, with a fourth in what used to be a smithy. Whether you're after a scone or a sausage sandwich (or both!) you're sure to find something to tempt you. Please keep in mind though that, in most teashops, it's best to change out of your muddy boots first.

Enjoy these walks in the Peak District but please let me offer some advice. I'd suggest you take an up to date OS map with you in case there have been any changes on the ground – you never know when a hedge may have been removed, or a tree felled. I'd also advise you to wear a good pair of boots and that you play it safe – the Peak District can be idyllic on a sunny day, but things can be very different on a wet and windy one. In fact, in some parts of the Peak District, you may get the sun, wind and rain all in the same morning! So be prepared, and don't tackle walks numbers 1, 4, 5 and 6 if there's any chance of the weather turning nasty.

It has been my great privilege over the last few months to revise and update these walks. I have been able to follow in my father's footsteps. I have seen the views he loved once again, and I have heard his voice in his descriptions of this beautiful area.

A few more walks with Dad … what son could ask for anything more? Enjoy your walking. *Jamie Wildgoose*

Walk 1
LANGSETT

*O*n *this walk you'll get the chance to visit North America – the farm, that is, or at least the remains of a farm. For those who didn't appreciate that the Peak District stretches this far north you are in for a lovely surprise because Langsett is a fascinating area. The only slight distraction is the distant drone (if you're on the moor) of the A616, but it's a minor one and even the wind turbines on the distant hills have a strange beauty of their own. The walk itself is a moderate one and shouldn't prove too taxing.*

It's nice to feel welcome in a tea room and that's certainly the case at the Bank View Café at Langsett. This is a traditional tea room, popular with walkers and cyclists, so you'll feel at home, though if you've got muddy boots on you may want to change them first.

There's a great choice of food including all day breakfasts (including a veggie breakfast) or if you're wanting a snack there are toasties, wraps and home-made soup. There are also some tasty sweets

available. There's even free wi-fi! Opening times are from 9am to 5pm every day except Christmas Day. Telephone: 01226 762337.
If the tea room is closed there's a pub opposite.

DISTANCE: 4¼ miles.
MAP: OS Explorer OL1 – The Peak District (Dark Peak Area).
STARTING POINT: Langsett (GR 211004).
HOW TO GET THERE: Langsett is 3¾ miles south-west of Penistone (as the crow flies) on the A616. The Peak Park car park (Langsett Barn) is on the southern side of the road. You can't miss it.

THE WALK

1. With your back to the main road, walk to the far right corner of the car park/picnic site where there is a choice of three routes to follow. Take the middle one, the public footpath, which at present has a green and yellow waymark with a 'B' in it. Walk alongside the wall on your left. Where the path splits, take the higher route inside the top side of the woodland. Initially there will be a wider bridleway over the wall on your right. Keep forward on the path ignoring any other paths to left and right (in particular a right turn towards a quarry). About a mile after leaving the car park, the path eventually descends to a bridleway with a concrete surface.

2. Turn right here into the woodland along the track. Some 300 yards later, where two bridleways meet, follow the bridleway left down the hill signposted, 'Public Bridleway to Swinden'. Proceed until a bridle-gate takes you out of Yorkshire Water's Access Land. Continue between the plantation on the left and a field on the right. Just beyond the end of the field swing left, still with the wood on your left. This brings you to an old stone outbuilding ('Swinden', according to the OS map). Turn left here through a wicket gate, into the woodland. Head forward, through the trees, descending gently to cross a small stream. Rise up the path to the point where you turned right at the beginning of this paragraph. Now turn right, downhill. Fifty yards later, on joining another path, turn right down to a stone bridge. The reservoir is visible to your left.

3. Cross the bridge and bear left on the track beyond. Follow this as it rises uphill and round to the right. You will soon be above the bridge (over the Little Don river) that you crossed ten or fifteen

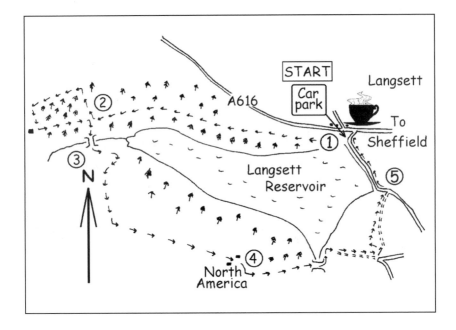

minutes earlier. Stay on the track to reach the corner of a fence. Keep straight along the track, rising across the moorland. Five hundred yards later (before reaching the crest of the hill) you arrive at a couple of stone stoops standing on their own. Fork left along the wide path through the heather. Stay on this for 600 yards to reach North America (the remains of a farm).

North America is, or was, North America Farm. In years gone by, farms were often called after faraway places and this is probably what happened here. When the reservoir was constructed at the start of the 20th century, the farms roundabout were all emptied as the water authority did not want the water destined for Sheffield to be polluted in any way. As a result, the family who lived here would have had to move on.

4. Pass through the gate beyond the ruins. The track descends and takes you beside trees on the left and the moorland on the right. Cross the bridge over Thickwoods Brook and follow the track as it bears round to the left before swinging right beyond a gate along a brick-surfaced track. This brings you to a gate with a concrete 'track' beyond. Head forward until you reach a road. Turn left here up the

All that remains of North America Farm

grassy track towards Upper Midhope. Some 130 yards later, on reaching some buildings, turn left across a concrete area. Ignore the bridleway on the right – continue for a further 20 yards to follow a path to the right beside a wall. This brings you to a stone track, which you should descend, ignoring paths into the wood on your left.

5. Turn left at the road and follow it over the reservoir embankment – take care though at the road corner just before the reservoir. On the far side of the reservoir wall proceed to the main road with the tea room directly opposite. Turn left up the main road for less than 200 yards – it may be safer walking on the pavement on the right. Ten yards before reaching Gilbert Hill on the right, follow the footpath on the left to get back to the car park.

Walk 2
BRADFIELD

Just a couple of miles inside the Peak Park boundary, Bradfield is associated with the largest burst dam disaster that ever happened in this country. It's a pity that it is linked with such a catastrophe for Bradfield is a quiet, rural area with attractive scenery. However, the valley still has its reservoirs – four of them: Strines, Dale Dike (now rebuilt), Agden and Damflask. Bradfield comprises Low Bradfield and High Bradfield. You park beside the cricket ground of Low Bradfield but High Bradfield, with its cobbled street, up the hill is well worth a visit later, especially the church. It is said that Robin Hood (otherwise, Robin of Loxley) came from these parts so you may be walking in his footsteps . The walk itself is a fairly easy one with just the one climb to Dungworth providing a challenge.

What could be nicer than a tea room in a garden centre? That's what you get at The Old Glasshouse and, whether you're stopping halfway round or coming back at the end of the walk, do take time to

12

browse. The Old Glasshouse is a very new development replacing the original café. There seems to be even more choice than there was, with toasted sandwiches (ham, cheese, tomato and onion) or, if you're looking for something more filling, specialities such as roast beef, red onion & Cheddar panini with salad garnish. There are also untoasted sandwiches, jacket potatoes, breakfast sandwiches/specialities and cakes. The Old Glasshouse opens from 9 am until 5 pm Mondays to Fridays, and 10 am until 5 pm at weekends. Telephone: 0114 2851487.

DISTANCE: 4¾ miles (includes the very short diversion to visit the teashop).
MAP: OS EXPLORER OL1 – The Peak District (Dark Peak Area).
STARTING POINT: Low Bradfield (GR 264919).
HOW TO GET THERE: If you're travelling from Derbyshire take the A57 from Ladybower towards Sheffield. Less than two miles later, turn left at the rather small sign for Strines Moor. Pass Strines Inn and after 1½ miles take the right turn for Bradfield. Descend into the valley and after another 1½ miles turn left for Low Bradfield, parking on the far side of the cricket ground.

THE WALK

1. Follow the road near Smithy Garage signposted 'Loxley'. Take the footpath on the right after 100 yards. Cross the watercourse and turn immediately left along the permissive path provided by Yorkshire Water. Follow this, ignoring all footpaths to the right, for the next 1¼ miles, with Damflask Reservoir on your left. Towards the end of this portion of the walk you'll be squeezed in between the reservoir on the left and the road on the right. When the path starts to bear left, look out for Oaks Lane (with a sign for 'Ughill') rising sharp right off the road you've been walking beside. At this point, leave Yorkshire Water's access land and walk on the pavement beside the main road. Eighty yards beyond Oaks Lane cross to, and ascend, the steep path on the right side of the road.

2. Continue uphill to a lane. Cross this, following the footpath opposite. In the first field aim for the wall corner above you, heading beyond it to the far corner of the field beside a wall on the left. On the road beyond, turn left into Dungworth, passing the carved stone as you enter the village inscribed with the intriguing words, 'My life, My love, My Children'. Ignore a right turn in Dungworth, taking a left turn afterwards, signed 'Storrs'. This lane bears left and then right past

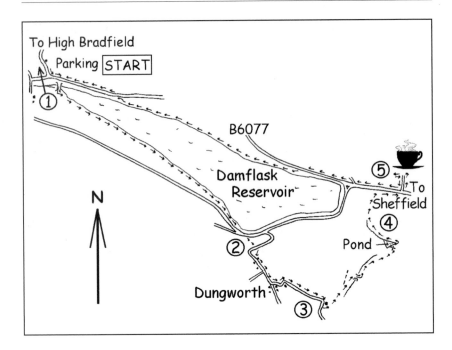

To High Bradfield
Parking START
① B6077
Damflask Reservoir
⑤ To Sheffield
N
② ④
Pond
Dungworth ③

some of the houses in the village. Some 200 yards past the last one, negotiate the sharp right-hand bend, turning left through a small gate immediately beyond the property on the corner.

Try to imagine the scene you would have witnessed if you had been walking down the road out of Dungworth, on a dark night in March 1864: Dale Dyke Dam further up the Loxley valley had just burst its banks. Tens of thousands of gallons of water came pouring downstream, sweeping everything before it. In total, over 240 men, women and children were killed that night, making it the worst ever damburst disaster in the history of this land.

3. Follow the path in front of the cottage and descend gradually down this valley, keeping the stream on your right. As the path levels out, cross the footbridge and turn immediately left to walk beside the stream which will now be on your left. With the stream still on your left, cross a step-over stile. Just beyond this, fork left immediately along the very bottom of the field to reach a squeezer stile. Pass through this into a small wood. On the far side turn left on to the path running downhill from the right. Ignore a path on the left after

Damflask Reservoir

20 yards that descends to a bridge. Proceed alongside the fence on your right to cross a substantial bridge over a watercourse. A large triangular pond is directly in front of you. Turn right here before turning sharp left at the end of the pond. The path then runs between the pond on the left and what appears to be a mill leat on the right.

☕ **4.** On reaching a weir, turn right alongside a stream. At the bridge made of wooden planks, turn right up to the main road. The Damflask Reservoir will be visible on your left as you go. At the main road turn right. After 175 yards turn left into West lane to reach Rhinegold Nurseries. Here's the tea stop! The café is towards the far end.

5. Retrace your steps to the main road and turn right. Continue along here (re-entering the Peak District) and ignore a left turn along the wall of the reservoir. Immediately before 'The Elders' on the right bear left onto the permissive path back to the side of the reservoir. Continue along here for about a mile, passing the sailing club. The path brings you back to the road, where you should turn left to return to Low Bradfield, taking care as you go.

Walk 3
LYME PARK

To all the ladies, an apology. You're unlikely to see Mr Darcy in the shape of Colin Firth bathing in the Mill Pond. For those who are unaware of the connection perhaps it should be mentioned that Lyme Park is where Pride And Prejudice *was filmed for the 1995 television series, with the Hall as Pemberley. This walk splits nicely into two, with the start and the finish largely in the parkland and the middle bit alongside the Macclesfield Canal. You should always have your camera with you when you go walking, but particularly today as there is plenty to see. The walk is a fairly moderate one.*

If you really want to enjoy the Timber Yard Coffee Shop at Lyme Park it may be best to avoid summer weekends. Who says so? The proprietor! It's so much quieter off-peak. It's definitely worth visiting though, and now the coffee shop is open all year and the summer opening hours are 10.30 am until 5 pm and the winter hours are 11 am until 4 pm. There's a Children's Choice menu, as well as scones, cakes (such as citrus cake) and soup with a roll and butter for the grown-ups. Or how do you fancy trying a barm cake filled with British bacon or Cumberland sausage? Telephone: 01663 762023.

If the tea room is closed then there are a couple of pubs in Disley and elsewhere along the A6.

DISTANCE: 4½ miles.
MAP: OS Explorer OL1 – The Peak District (Dark Peak Area).
STARTING POINT: Lyme Park (GR 963824).
HOW TO GET THERE: Lyme Park is on the A6 between Disley and High Lane. Once you've left the A6 you've got a 1½ mile drive to the National Trust car park. There's a fee payable unless you're a National Trust member.

THE WALK

1. From the car park, walk to the tarmac access road between the car park and the Mill Pond. With the pond in front of you turn left along the road. Ignore all paths on the right in the vicinity of the pond. With Lyme Hall away to your left ignore a path on the left rising uphill. Some 200 yards beyond this path, fork right on a tarmac lane then, 100 yards later, right again to walk beside a high stone wall on the right. A wide view of the Cheshire Plain opens out ahead of you. After 300 yards turn right to cross a ladder stile. Walk along the top side of three fields to reach a tarmac driveway.

2. Turn left to walk towards Plattwood Farm. Keep on the right side of the buildings before taking the first right to walk down a track with Platt Wood itself on your left. Pass Plattwood Cottages on the left. Stay on the track beyond. When a track leads right to another redbrick cottage, ignore this, continuing along the track ahead. Ignore a path that crosses the track. Where the track appears to be heading into a farmyard, swing right and pass Middlecale Cottages. You then cross the Macclesfield Canal. Keep right to reach the canal itself.

3. Turn right along the canal and keep this on your left for the next 1¼ miles.

As you go, you are likely to pass a variety of narrowboats with names like Wagtail, Sandpiper and Rowan. You'll also see, away to your left, the high ground above Lyme Park. The Macclesfield Canal runs from the Peak Forest

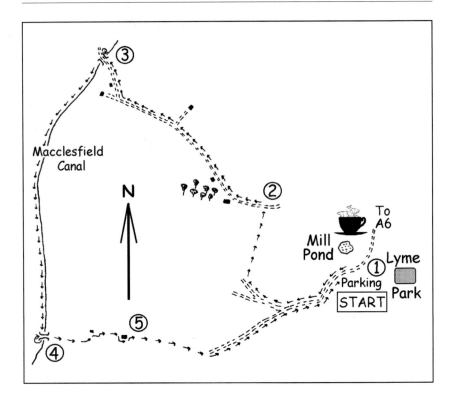

Canal for just over 26 miles to join up with the Trent and Mersey Canal. It was built in the 1830s – a bit later than many other canals; as by this time the railways were starting to have an impact on the shifting of goods around the country, the canal was not a particularly successful business undertaking.

On reaching the Trading Post you may be able to get a cup of tea. After passing under bridge number 16 keep right to cross it, though you may wish to continue for a few more yards to take the opportunity to enjoy a rest on a seat by the side of the canal.

4. After crossing the bridge, bear half-right to a kissing gate. Beyond this, bear half-left, walking up the side of the field towards the house on the hillside. In the top left corner of the field, ignore the first stile on the left, and pass through the kissing gate in the corner. Keep on the left side of the field beyond, walking up the hedgeside to pass through the kissing gate. Follow the path to reach a tarmac drive

The Macclesfield Canal

descending from the right. Follow this uphill. Pass the Peak & Northern sign (no. 221) on the left and head towards the house ahead, turning right on the tarmac in front of it. At the point where you can turn right along the driveway away from the buildings or left towards them, turn left for a few yards only. Then turn right through a gate. Now head forward to pass between the large building (made of corrugated sheets) and the stone building to its left. Keep forward for a few yards before turning right. Then cross a stile, then a ladder stile after 10 yards to re-enter both Lyme Park and the Peak Park.

The house in Lyme Park is spectacular when viewed across the lake and well worth visiting after your walk. It is a much older house than it looks, having been altered by a Venetian architect. With its attractive gardens surrounded by 1,400 acres of ancient deer park it is hard to believe Stockport is just down the road.

5. Walk directly up the hill beside the fence. After 275 yards you reach the top of this climb. On the other side of it is a parking area. Find your way down to this and turn left on the tarmac road to return to the car park, ignoring a left fork as you go.

Walk 4
CASTLETON

Castleton is a honeypot with plenty of sights to see. You can explore them later though. Before that you'll have a challenging climb up to Hollins Cross that will get the heart beating. Then you rise up more steadily to Mam Tor. On the trek back a path descending through Cave Dale gives excellent views of Peveril Castle before you pass through a nick in the rocks and find yourself almost magically back in the 21st century. Please remember – though full of stunning views, this is quite a testing walk.

This family-run business, Rose Cottage, on the main street of Castleton, is well worth a visit, with the family priding themselves on their produce – cakes, pies, scones and desserts – the majority homemade. There's also a lovely garden area now open, weather permitting, where you can take a dog if you want to. There's plenty to sample at Rose Cottage, such as beer battered cod or grilled gammon. There's a specials board with inviting dishes such as savoury pie and open omelette with pancetta, peas, and goats cheese, topped with dressed rocket. There are some tasty homemade cakes too. The carrot cake in particular! Rose Cottage opens from 10 am until 5 pm all week but closes on Friday. In summer it may open longer. We're running out of space – and you will too! Telephone: 01433 620472.

If Rose Cottage is closed, there are a number of other tea rooms and pubs in Castleton.

DISTANCE: 6¼ miles.
MAP: OS Explorer OL1 – The Peak District (Dark Peak Area).
STARTING POINT: Castleton (GR 148830).
HOW TO GET THERE: As you enter Castleton along the A6187 from the east, keep on through the village and the car park is at the western end, clearly signposted.

THE WALK

1. As you entered the car park you may have noticed a stream running along the right-hand side of it. Walk to this stream, turn left alongside it and follow it downstream to the end of the car park. Once there, walk straight forward between houses and a larger stream until you come to a lane descending gently from the right. Turn left along this lane. This is Millbridge. Cross a stream. Ignore a lane forking left just beyond this. Pass the cemetery to come out into open country. Ignore a track to the right.

Ahead, one of the most famous ridge walks in England is visible. The track between Mam Tor and Losehill has therefore suffered more than its fair share of wear and tear, but more of that later. Winnats Pass is visible to the left – a deep cleft in the landscape renowned as the scene of the murder of two lovers who were eloping some centuries ago.

At a T-junction turn left and stay on the track as it passes between hedges. It is now known as Hollowford Road. The climb looms ever nearer. The track (now surfaced in tarmac) rises gently. When it swings left, on a rougher track with no public access, pass through the swing gate and keep forward up the stony track to reach open (and steeper!) ground.

2. Bear left up the clearly beaten path and stay on this to reach Hollins Cross at the top of the ridge. In the valley beyond is Edale. If you stop

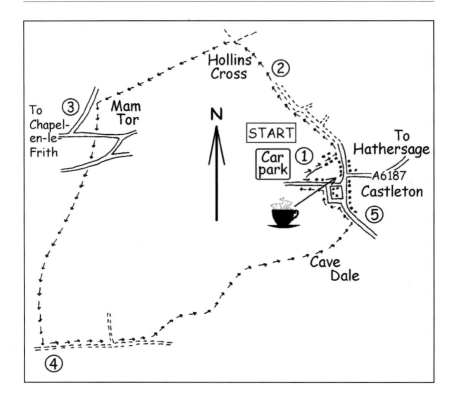

here for a chocolate bar or a sandwich, beware the sheep! Turn left along the ridge towards Mam Tor.

You'll be walking on old flagstones laid by Peak Park Rangers. The flagstones were brought in by helicopter after originally being quarried near Holmfirth. It is hoped that this will cut down the erosion of the most popular upland walking route in the Peak District. As you reach Mam Tor you'll see evidence of the ditches that form part of an ancient hill-fort. According to the information point Mam Tor was the 'Mother Hill'. The modern day may intrude hereabouts as it is a favourite spot for paragliders to take off.

Pass the trig point on the right to descend the path to the road.

3. At the road turn left down the steps beside the fence to walk towards a grassy, disused quarry some 400 or 500 yards away with a line of trees beyond. Reach (and cross) a lane to follow the path for

Windy Knoll. Proceed forward, keeping to the right of the quarry. Stay on the track to reach another road. Ignore a ladder stile slightly to the left; bear right to pass through a gate. Stay on the tarmac access road for no more than 15 yards before bearing half-right along the wide grassy path. Aim towards a wall heading up the hillside ahead. Once you reach it walk beside it until you reach a stony track half a mile later.

4. Turn left along the track. Proceed and pass through a stile by a gate, then negotiate a step-over stile. Follow the walled track straight ahead. Climb another step-over, immediately turning left over yet another and proceed through the short, narrow, walled enclosure. Beyond this bear one-third right towards Win Hill, the 'pimple' on the skyline.

You're now on the Limestone Way, which runs (the other way!) to Rocester in Staffordshire, some 45 miles away. The route was created by Matlock Rotary Club and provides many walkers with an excellent route to link the north of Derbyshire with the south.

Across the field, in a shallowish valley, resist the temptation to continue forward along the rising track – bear right to pass through a wooden bridle-gate 80 yards away. Follow the valley-bottom path now for a mile. Initially this is a grassy descent, becoming bumpier (and stonier) as you go. In some places the stones underfoot will require that you take care, but the views of Cave Dale (which you are descending) make it all worthwhile.

After some distance the ruins of Peveril Castle are visible on your left. The castle was built in Norman times for William the Conqueror's illegitimate son, William Peveril. It is now in the care of English Heritage and open all year round from Wednesday to Sunday.

Eventually you leave the dale via a nick in the rocks and you're back in Castleton!

☕ **5.** Proceed forward between cottages to turn left down Bargate. Keep to the left of the war memorial, before bearing right in front of the youth hostel down Castle Street. At the main street turn left to the car park or right to the tea rooms.

23

Walk 5
HATHERSAGE

Hathersage is probably most famous for its association with two well-known historical characters – Charlotte Brontë and Little John. Miss Brontë was friendly with the family of the then vicar of Hathersage and rumour has it that she based Thornfield Hall (from Jane Eyre*) on North Lees Hall, which you will pass as you head back to Hathersage. As regards Little John, he was Robin Hood's right-hand man and also, apparently, an 'athersidge lad dwelling at the time of his death in a cottage next to the churchyard. The walk? A gentle, steady, climb that leads up to Stanage Edge before a gentle, steady, descent brings you back again – passing North Lees Hall as you go. A chance to enjoy some truly inspirational countryside.*

The Pool Café is on the opposite side of the road from the car park, near the swimming pool. There's a good choice of tasty food – vegetarian breakfast, hot sandwiches (bacon, sausage, egg or tomatoes or a combination) and 9 inch pizzas. There are main courses too – steak or chicken pie or homemade chilli with rice. There are vegetarian dishes such as broccoli and cheese bake, as well as fish – freshly battered cod or haddock. Walkers, climbers and cyclists are all welcome with the Pool Café opening at 8 am every day and they stay open until at least 6 pm. The Pool Café even has its own Facebook page! Telephone: 01433 651159.

There are other tea rooms and pubs to choose from in Hathersage if the Pool Café is closed.

DISTANCE: 5¾ miles.
MAP: OS Explorer OL1 – The Peak District (Dark Peak Area).
STARTING POINT: Hathersage (GR 231814).
HOW TO GET THERE: If you are travelling from Grindleford along the B6001, the car park is signposted on the right, shortly after entering Hathersage.

THE WALK

1. Turn left on the road between the car park and the Pool Café. Where the road bends right, keep forward through Ibbotsons Croft along the pavement on the right. Cross the main road to walk along Baulk Lane for ¾ mile. Initially, you pass the church away to the right. Ignore all footpaths off the lane as it rises steadily up the valley ahead. The high ground of Stanage Edge will be visible 1½ miles away. Two hundred yards before you reach Cowclose, fork left off the track to reach a wicket gate. Proceed on the tarmac path beyond. Brookfield Manor is on your left. Keep to the right of the last few buildings to cross Hood Brook. Beyond this swing right to Birley Lane. The cottage to the right is known as Brontë Cottage.

2. Cross the lane and follow the path for Green's House, initially through the middle of the field. Pass through a gate into a delightful wood (The Warren) with a stream on your left. Fork left over the stream via a delightful wooden bridge. Keep forward and pass through a narrow gate into a field. Continue rising, to another gate ahead. Keep in the same direction in the next field to a step-stile to the right of Green's House. At the end of the path you reach a track. Turn left immediately to walk through the yard of Green's House. After 30 yards turn right through a gate to proceed on a walled path. Stay on this (alongside a wall on your right) as it enters open moorland. Pass through a gateway in the wall, keeping beside the wall (now on your left) and climb a stone step-stile. Continue alongside the wall on your left to reach a lane. Impressive views abound.

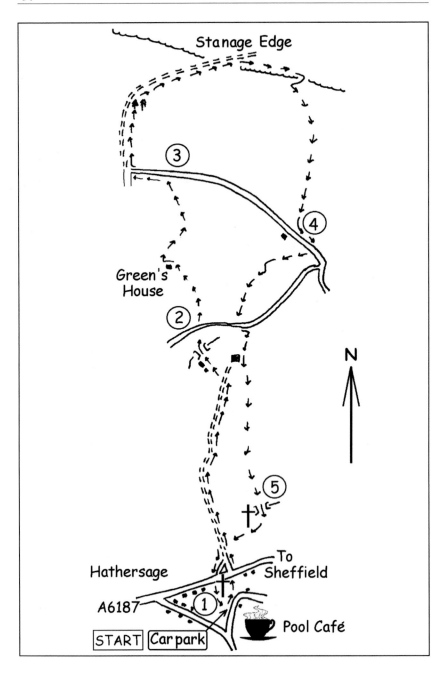

Stanage Edge

③

④

Green's
House

②

N

⑤

Hathersage

To
Sheffield

A6187

①

START Car park

Pool Café

Walking towards Hathersage

3. Turn left at the lane, over the cattle grid, then 200 yards later, at a T-junction, turn right along a track. Follow this, swinging right as you go up to Stanage Edge. As you proceed you may be able to see Hathersage church in the valley bottom. Where the track starts to move away from the Edge, bear right along the bridleway, which stays near to the Edge. After 200 yards, with a rocky outcrop immediately to your left, turn sharp right to zigzag downhill off the Edge. This paved path soon loses height as you pick your way between the rocks. After passing beneath some trees you come out into the open. With a car park away to your right, fork left off the path to follow a grassy path heading towards a small, stone building in the trees. It's a toilet block!

4. At the lane, turn left and continue for 100 yards or so until, just before a right-hand bend, you turn sharp right down a track with a stream below to your left. In the open field continue to descend on the track. Pass through a farm gate with North Lees Hall directly beyond. Turn sharp left after a few yards, keeping the hall on your right.

North Lees Hall was believed to have been built at the end of the 16th century. One family who lived hereabouts were the Eyres and the rest, as they say, is history. Charlotte Brontë visited Hathersage at that time and subsequently wrote Jane Eyre, *using North Lees Hall as the model for Thornfield Hall in the book.*

Proceed down the tarmac driveway to the lane. Turn left, continuing for 75 yards to pass the campsite entrance on your left. Turn right up the banking and go through the wicket gate. Follow the grassy path towards Cowclose. With the stone farm buildings to your right, pass through a wicket gate immediately to the left of the building with a breeze-block wall. Proceed and pass through a farm gate to rise up the right-hand side of the field beyond. Stay on the bottom side of this and a second field. Some distance later, cross the stile at the end of the field. Proceed along the path between hedges before bearing slightly right towards the mast on the horizon. This leads to the bottom side of the field, where you should turn left, heading in the general direction of the church.

☕ **5.** Cross a small bridge over a stream and ascend to the top-right corner of the field. Bear right beyond to a road. Walk along this, keeping the churchyard to your right. Turn right through the lychgate and walk forward. Just before the church porch look to the left for Little John's grave. Continue through the churchyard to reach the edge of it. At the kissing gate turn left then immediately right to walk down beside the wall to Baulk Lane. Turn left along this. Subsequently bear right down Besom Lane to reach the main road. Cross to the Methodist church grounds and, keeping the church on your left, walk through these to pick up a path which leads back into the car park.

Walk 6
LONGSHAW

*T*he National Trust is one of the largest landowners in the country and it owns great swathes of the Peak District. Much of this walk passes through its property – stunning Dark Peak scenery where you can suffer misty dark days or revel in clear blue skies. This is an enjoyable (though fairly testing) walk in most weathers and in all seasons, with some fascinating points of interest (Longshaw Lodge, Padley Chapel and Winyard's Nick) thrown in for good measure.

 The building that houses Longshaw Lodge Tea Room is part National Trust shop and part tea room – a nice place to rest after the walk and revitalise yourself. You can choose something fairly substantial from the menu or opt for a piece of cake if you prefer. So, what to choose? If you've got a good appetite you could try soup of the day with a roll or a traditional Derbyshire oatcake with cheese and tomato filling. There are people from Derbyshire who live outside the county who stock up on oatcakes when they come back home because they can't get them in 'foreign' parts. What about something a bit different – Homity Pie perhaps? These are all homemade. *And*, there are delicious cakes such as lemon drizzle and chocolate. The tea room is open every weekend all year. For most of March until the end of October it's open all week. The tea room usually opens at 10.30 am and closes at 5 pm (4 pm in winter). Closed Christmas Eve and Christmas Day. Telephone: 01433 637904.

Try Fox House Inn if the tea room is closed. There are also pubs and tea rooms in Hathersage.

DISTANCE: 5½ miles.
MAPS: OS Explorer OL1 – The Peak District (Dark Peak Area) and OS Explorer OL24 (White Peak Area).
STARTING POINT: Longshaw Lodge (GR 267801).
HOW TO GET THERE: Proceed along the B6521 from Grindleford to reach the main road (the A6187). Turn right, then right again at Fox House Inn. The National Trust car park is 150 yards further on, on the right.

THE WALK

1. Walk downhill to the bottom of the car park. Continue down the gravel path beyond. Cross a stream then turn right for the Visitor Centre. On reaching a level drive cross over and follow the footpath down some steps. The path now passes in front of the Visitor Centre and Longshaw Lodge on your left.

The Lodge, though a National Trust property, is not open to the public, being rented apartments. It was originally a hunting and shooting lodge for the Dukes of Rutland.

After passing through a gate you'll find yourself under five yew trees. Turn right down a gravel path and continue until you reach a pond.

2. Stay on the path as it runs alongside the pond on your right. Eventually the pond is left behind and (after ignoring a path to the left) you reach the main road. Cross this and pass through a wicket gate. Take the path leading to the footbridge and turn left beyond, beside Burbage Brook. With the brook immediately on your left continue until the waters cascade to a lower level through the large rocks. Proceed along the footpath ahead into the trees. You should be

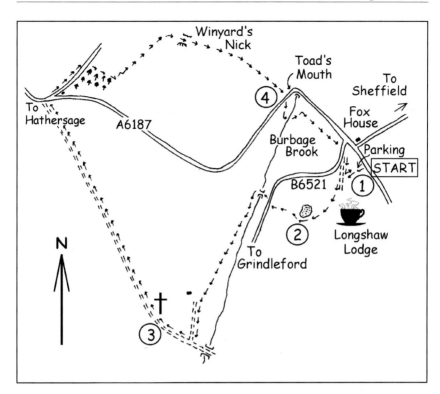

able to see the brook to your left, below, for some distance. Stay on the main path, ignoring all lesser paths to the left that descend into the gorge. About ½ mile after entering the wood, the main path you're on starts to rise but ¼ mile later you'll find you're descending again and passing a low, stone building with curved roof on the right. The path brings you to a gate. Beyond this descend the gravel track to another track at the bottom. Turn right then.

3. Proceed along this to pass Brunts Barn and Padley Chapel to re-enter the Longshaw Estate.

Padley Chapel is all that remains of Padley Hall. It was hereabouts that the Padley Martyrs (two Catholic priests, Nicholas Garlick and Robert Ludlam) were arrested in the late 16th century before being taken to Derby and tried. They were subsequently hanged, drawn and quartered near St Mary's Bridge. A pilgrimage takes place each year to the chapel.

31

Stay on the main track past a number of houses on the left. Keep on this track as it rises steadily for the best part of a mile, passing first one then a second property on the left. Eventually you reach the A6187 which descends into Hathersage. Take time to recover, whilst admiring the view. Turn right up the road. After 60 yards, take care as you fork left on the minor road to the left of the house dated 1844. Proceed alongside Whim Wood. At the end of the wood turn right into the trees. Proceed away from the road beside a wall on your left. Pass through a gate to leave the wood. Walk up the slope in front and turn left on the grassy track. Twenty yards beyond an unusual stone building bear right. After a further 15 yards turn left along a narrow path to go through a small gate onto privately owned land with public access. This was very overgrown at the time we did the walk. Walk straight forward (with a wall down to your left) towards the two rocky outcrops, 'Winyard's Nick', 500 yards ahead. On joining another path bear left along it, now aiming slightly left of Winyard's Nick. With the 'Nick' immediately to your right, turn right at the largish flat stone to walk through the hollow between the two outcrops. Where the path you're on levels out, it is crossed by another – ignore this – proceed forward, walking downhill towards the road over ½ mile away. As you go, to the left is Carl Wark (an ancient hill-fort) and to the left of that (and higher than it), Higger Tor. Ignore all cross-paths. When you find yourself levelling out on a grassy path, keep straight on. You should reach the A625 50 yards or so to the right of Toad's Mouth. If you wish to have a closer look at Toad's Mouth, an unusual shaped rock perched just above the road, cross the road and turn left to walk towards the road-bend.

4. Return to the point where you crossed the road. Pass through the wicket gate into the Longshaw Estate. Walk towards Burbage Brook ahead by forking right a few yards after leaving the road. Cross the bridge over the brook and follow the paved footpath beyond. After crossing a small stream turn right, crossing it again. Stay on the main path, ignoring all paths to the left. On reaching the road after ¼ mile, turn right before forking almost immediately left through the gateway opposite. Note the old guidepost on the right and see what you can decipher. Continue along the drive towards Longshaw Lodge to reach the Visitor Centre, where there are some toilets too. After visiting the Visitor Centre return the way you came back to the car park.

Walk 7
TIDESWELL

A *walk full of contrasts and interest, including a path through the allotments! Tideswell, with its impressive church, 'the Cathedral of the Peak', is an attractive small town full of character. Initially you'll wind your way through its streets before heading out along Manchester Road to reach Brook Bottom. Then an old track (Water Lane) leads you onto higher ground and the quiet village of Wheston. You then descend to pick your way through Peter Dale, where you'll follow the Limestone Way. You stay on this for a couple of miles before leaving it behind you to find that path through the allotments. This in turn leads to the remains of the 15th-century Butterton Cross.*

 The Vanilla Kitchen in Tideswell was originally an old joiner's shop which became a tea room (the Hills 'n' Dales) in March 1988, and you'll be pleased it did. There's a friendly atmosphere with plenty of choice. Whether you're wanting a breakfast plate (with 2 sausages, 2 fried eggs, bacon, beans, mushrooms, tomatoes, black pudding and toast (a veggie breakfast is also available) or something simpler such as a jacket potato, Vanilla Kitchen will suit you. There's a specials board with tempting items such as cottage pie with vegetables, or steak and ale pie which is their signature dish, and hand-cut chips catching the eye. Okay it may have a few more calories than you'd want to consume but you've earned it. Talking of calories there are some very tasty cakes including homemade jumbo scones with jam and cream. If you're a coffee drinker, then you might be tempted by a macchiato or a baby chino sprinkled with chocolate and marshmallows. Telephone: 01298 871519. The Vanilla Kitchen is open 7 days a week in summer and 5 in winter (closed Mondays and Tuesdays in winter).

If the Vanilla Kitchen is closed, there are a couple of pubs where you may be able to get something to eat, depending on the time of day.

DISTANCE: 6¼ miles.

MAP: OS Explorer OL24 – The Peak District (White Peak Area).

STARTING POINT: Tideswell (GR 152755).

HOW TO GET THERE: From the A623 north of Tideswell, drive south-westwards into the village. Keep on the main street past the church. The road bears right, then left, before widening. Park in this area; the Catholic church should be on your left.

THE WALK

1. From your car head along the main street towards the Parish Church of St John the Baptist, passing the Vanilla Kitchen as you go. Continue past the church, turning left immediately beyond the George Inn. Rise uphill to the primary school. Pass this but, just beyond, at a hollow in the road, turn left down a short road (St John's Road). Turn right at the bottom. You soon pass the impressive Bagshaw Hall on the left. Continue on the main road, passing Market Square on the right. Ignore the left turn to Wheston. After 350 yards look out on the right for Manchester Road Well – originally a source of drinking water for local residents. Continue along Manchester Road for ⅓ mile to reach Brook Villa on the left. After 150 yards turn left over the stream.

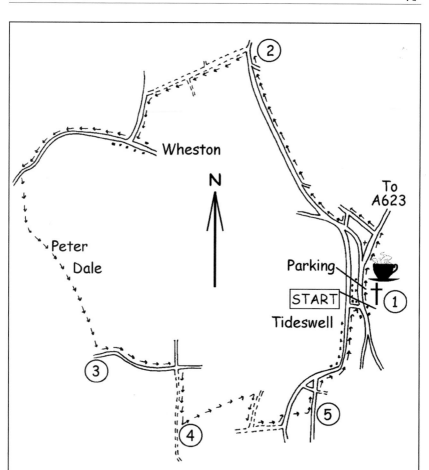

This is Brook Bottom and has for centuries been a watering place; the track you will follow is known as Water Lane.

2. Walk up the stony track away from the road. Stay on this, ignoring a right turn then a left to reach a tarmac lane after ¾ mile. Turn left to descend into Wheston.

The village of Wheston is very different from its neighbour, Tideswell. It's a quiet mainly agricultural village and just downhill from Wheston Hall Farm is one of the best preserved ancient crosses in Derbyshire- over 600 years old.

Turn right through Wheston and stay on the lane as it eventually descends to Dale Head. As the lane descends the scenery changes quite noticeably. To the right is Hay Dale, to the left Peter Dale. Cross the stile on your left into the latter (it may be signposted 'Limestone Way'). Continue through the bottom of the dale for approximately 1 mile. After the smooth and easy road-walking this may prove rather more of a test, as the dale can be rocky in places (and wet and muddy too, depending on the season!).

3. Eventually you reach a lane. According to a noticeboard that used to stand at the lane a hidden tunnel supposedly links the dale you've just walked through with Tideswell itself. Turn left up the hill. A steady climb brings you to a crossroads. Take the right turn along the walled track. Stay on this for just over 500 yards, passing one footpath on the left (with Peak & Northern signpost No. 217 pointing the way) to cross a second one on the left. You will need to keep your wits about you here. The step-over stile you need is just 40 yards *before* a largish tree ahead of you on the right. It's the tallest tree around so unless it's been cut down you should be OK!

4. Keep on the right-hand side of the long field to cross a stile. Bear slightly right to the stile on the left-hand side of the farm gate at the top of the second field. Turn right on to the track beyond. This leads you downhill. Ignore a private road to the left. At the T-junction of tracks turn left, ignoring a track to the right after a while. At a narrow tarmac lane turn left, then right onto the path through the allotments! At the lane on the far side the route turns left but if you turn right for 30 yards you reach a double farm gate. Four yards beyond this, in the wall, is the remains of Butterton Cross.

5. Return to the main route. Keep forward when the lane you're on is crossed by another. You then reach a T-junction. Turn right in front of some bungalows. Follow this road, ignoring all roads off it. Eventually, turn right down Sunnybank Lane. This leads to the main street and your car.

Walk 8
EYAM

A flattish walk from the plague village of Eyam, which cut itself off in 1666 in order to prevent the disease, which had spread there from London and was so badly ravaging the village, being spread to neighbouring villages. The route heads across the fields to Foolow with its village pond and roaming ducks before you reach the hamlet of Grindlow. After that you'll get the chance to walk down Silly Dale before returning to Eyam along field paths and stony Tideswell Lane. A walk you can tackle without exerting yourself too much! Incidentally, the locals call the village 'Eem' not 'Ee-am'.

The Buttery forms part of the Eyam Hall Craft Centre and you're bound to find something a little different. There is homemade quiche and ham and pork pie with salad, soft roll and butter and sandwiches with various fillings with salad garnish and potato crisps, the Buttery should be able to replenish you after walking around Eyam and Stoney Middleton. Then there are toasties and jackets with salad, or perhaps you'd like something warming like homemade soup – perhaps tomato and fresh basil? Then there are some delicious cakes. The Buttery is open from 10.30 am until 4.30 pm. In the winter the Buttery is open from Tuesday to Sunday and, in the months of November, December and January, it is open from Wednesday to Sunday. Telephone: 01433 630505.

If the Buttery is closed, there are a number of other teashops (and a pub further down the village).

DISTANCE: 6¼ miles.
MAP: OS Explorer OL24 – The Peak District (White Peak Area).
STARTING POINT: Eyam (GR 216767).
HOW TO GET THERE: Follow the A623 north-westwards from Baslow. Cross the traffic lights at Calver. Two miles later turn right on the B6521 for Eyam. Follow the 'Eyam Museum' signs. The car park is opposite the museum.

THE WALK
1. From the car park entrance turn left downhill. Pass Hall Hill Troughs. At the T-junction turn right and follow the road for 250 yards, passing various information boards relating to the history of Eyam.

Eyam is known as the Plague Village. Legend has it that a piece of cloth from London carried plague-riddled fleas. Before long the plague had taken hold in the village and at the suggestion of William Mompesson, the church minister, Eyam people put themselves in quarantine to stop the disease spreading to neighbouring villages. People buried their dead near their homes as there were no church services. The Riley graves outside the village contain the bodies of a father and his six children. His wife survived and presumably buried all of them.

Turn left into Tideswell Lane. Ignore a lane forking left after 175 yards. Take the path on the right immediately beyond the house called Scrumpy Croft (formerly Craig y Don). Pass into a field, heading forward to a wicket gate. Proceed to a stile at a wall corner. Beyond this keep alongside the wall on your left. With a ruined building on your right, pass through a gap in the tumbled-down wall and continue with another wall on your left. Cross a narrow field. Keep forward in the next field to a squeezer ahead. Foolow should be visible by now. Keep forward in the field with the small hillocks (old lead workings). Cross a track. Proceed on the right side of the wall in front. At the end of the wall proceed to the small gate ahead. This leads into a field with

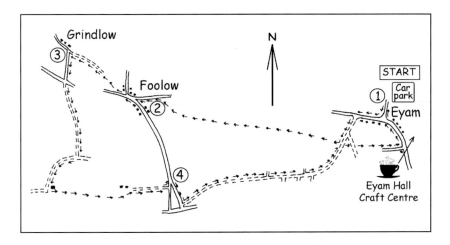

more of the grassy hillocks. Here care is needed! Bear slightly left to a squeezer 10 yards in front of a water trough (it will be out of sight initially!). Keep in the same direction in the next field to pass through a tumbled-down wall. Then, heading towards the left-hand side of the main group of the buildings of Foolow, descend into and then out of Linen Dale. Once out of the dale walk alongside the wall on your left to reach a tumbled-down building. At the small gate a few yards beyond this bear half-right to the road. Turn left along this into Foolow.

2. As you enter Foolow, stay on the main road to reach the village green complete with 14th-century cross ('… erected in its present position in 1868'), village pond and an old well beyond that. Leave Foolow by the main road. One hundred and fifty yards beyond the last house, take the footpath on the right. Pass through the clear stiles in the first two fields, heading the slightest touch left to cross the third one. Here you join a track which leads all the way to the edge of Grindlow where you may see some of the gliders from the local gliding club.

3. At the road leading into Grindlow, turn left (unless you want to turn right to look at Grindlow itself). At the T-junction 350 yards further on cross straight over towards the bungalow ahead. Follow the walled track that dips down to the left of this building. This leads you into the interestingly named Silly Dale! Stay on the track for about

½ mile until it reaches a T-junction of tracks. Take the right turn to reach Stanley House Farm. Where the driveway turns right, cross the stepover stile on the left immediately beyond the farm. Keep forward, with the wall on your left, for four fields. Look over your right shoulder for a view of Peter's Stone in Cressbrookdale. The rocky outcrop was the site of the last gibbeting in Derbyshire. At the end of the fourth field the stile is to the right of the left-hand corner of the field. Beyond this head *slightly* right to a stile beside a gate. Once again proceed through a number of fields with the wall on your left. With Brosterfield Farm on your left bear left to the far left corner of the field, where a stile leads you onto the driveway. Turn right here to proceed to the road.

☕ **4.** At the road turn left and almost immediately right. Three hundred yards on, after passing Dale Head House (1902) and immediately before the main road, turn left down Tideswell Lane. Stay on this, ignoring all tracks off it for 1½ miles. Eventually you come back to the path you took at Scrumpy Croft. Turn right here. Cross the paddock and take the path on the opposite side of the lane. Keep straight forward then walk between the houses to join a road which leads directly to Eyam Hall Craft Centre. In front of the craft centre turn left and then right into Hawkhill Road and back to the start.

Foolow

Walk 9
CALVER

*W*ithin *10 minutes of leaving the hustle and bustle of Calver you'll be rising up towards Longstone Edge. As you climb higher the views grow and eventually you're there. You'll soon realise that Longstone Edge is very different from Curbar and Baslow Edges on the other side of the valley: they are impressive 'cliffs' of dark sandstone beloved by climbers; Longstone Edge is a three-mile long, rounded, grassy ridge usually showing signs of being plundered for its minerals. Indeed, that is the thing that you'll probably notice most – the quarrying. But bear with us as you walk down towards Coombs Dale and later, in the dale itself, you'll realise that it's an impressive area that sometimes gives rise to flights of imagination – is that Black Harry sitting astride a stallion at the top of the dale?*

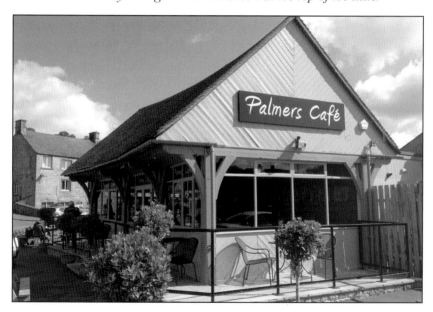

Popular with local walkers and cyclists alike, there's plenty of choice on offer at Palmer's Café, including a large breakfast – 10 items, or a small breakfast – 5 items. I can recommend the small version after this walk in autumn or winter. I didn't quite have the courage to try the large one! You may fancy some panini – ham and pineapple, cheese and onion or cheese and bacon, perhaps. For something out of the ordinary, try a Derbyshire oatie with salad and a filling of cheddar and mushroom or Wensleydale and apricot. In the cakes section the portions of flapjack caramel crisp are very generous – you might want to share one. There are toasties and jacket potatoes on the menu too. The café is open from 8.30 am to 5.30 pm seven days a week. There is also free wi-fi for customers. Telephone: 01433 639931.

If the café is closed, there's the Derwentwater Arms down the road near the spot where you probably parked your car.

DISTANCE: 5¼ miles.
MAP: OS Explorer OL24 – The Peak District (White Peak Area).
STARTING POINT: Calver (GR 240747).
HOW TO GET THERE: Travelling northwards along the A623 from Baslow you reach the traffic lights at Calver crossroads. Turn left here as though you're heading to Bakewell. Then turn immediately left into Sough Lane. Park down near the cricket ground where the road is wider.

THE WALK

1. Walk back to the crossroads. Turn left along the Bakewell road. Immediately beyond the garden centre turn right onto the footpath for Great Longstone. Proceed up the tarmac drive, continuing forward on the fenced track as the drive bears left towards a house. Cross a stile at the end of the fenced section. Continue along the path ahead as it rises slowly until you're walking beside a wall. Good views open out on your right. Ignore a path on the left before passing through a gate onto a tree-lined track which is delightful when the sun slants through the trees onto it. Ignore a footpath to the right at this gate.

2. Ascend the track for some distance. Ignore all gateways on both sides of the path. The views will widen out with Eyam Edge a couple of miles away to your right. The nearer you get to the top of this climb, the more gradual the slope. On reaching the end of the walled track you will see a number of enclosures; pass through the small wicket gate in front of you. Proceed up the left side of the field ahead along the grassy path, pass through another wicket gate and stay on the left

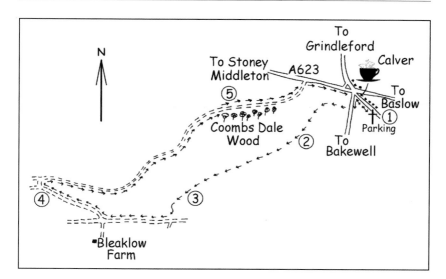

side of the field beyond this. You will then start to descend slightly before reaching a gate across the track.

3. Walk up the track beyond the gate into the gorse and bracken. Ignore a track to the left 100 yards further on. Keep forward along the stony track you're on bearing slightly right, then left, then right again. As the track starts to rise and swing more noticeably right, take the footpath on the left alongside a fence. This brings you to a wide stony track. Turn right along this for half a mile, alongside a narrow strip of trees on the left. At the entrance to Bleaklow Farm on the left, turn right. With your back to the farm drive (and with an outbuilding in the field 100 yards in front of you) bear half-left to follow a sandy track (after passing through a bridle-gate) which can be seen disappearing over a rise in the ground. Do not turn hard left into the quarry workings! Follow the sandy track, with a wall on your right, for about ¾ mile. As you proceed it becomes a narrow, walled, green lane. Down to your right is Coombs Dale, through which you will shortly be walking.

4. After crossing a (sometimes muddy) access road, pass through a bridle-gate and turn right immediately. Pass through another bridle-gate 30 yards further on. This brings you to the area known as Black Harry Gate, Black Harry being a notorious highwayman who used to frequent these parts! Nothing else seems to be known of him – another story lost in the mists of time. Turn right to follow the track down the dale for 2 miles. Ignore all paths to left and right.

About halfway down the dale look out on the right for Sallet Hole Mine. This goes straight into the hillside for approximately half a mile. There are many people alive who have worked down this mine and they can tell of the different levels that were worked for minerals and of the accidents that happened there. It comes as something of a surprise to learn that mining like this still takes place within the Peak Park. We sometimes forget it is a working landscape and that residents have to make a living- a difficult balancing act for the National Park Authority.

By the time you reach the Peak Park's Coombsdale Wood the path will be level and well-surfaced, but before that it resembles a stream bed in part, though it appears there are plans to improve the surface.

5. With Coombsdale Wood on your right continue along the valley bottom path until it swings left to take you past the playing fields on your left and out onto the A623. Turn right along the road to the crossroads to reach Palmers Café, then your car.

The path signed 'Great Longstone'

44

Walk 10
MONSAL HEAD

*If you can come up with a better placed teashop than Hobb's Café &
Craft Centre then let me know. It stands overlooking one of the most
photographed views in the Peak District, Monsal Dale with its viaduct. This
may be a short walk but it's a strenuous one, as no sooner have you walked
down to the River Wye than you're climbing up the other side of it – to enjoy
the views. The unusually named farm Brushfield Hough is soon passed
before you descend into the dale once again before getting the chance to
walk near the river for a mile or so. Then, a steady climb takes you
back up to Monsal Head and the teashop.*

 Hobb's Café must be in one of the best spots in the Peak District.
The only downside must be the number of visitors who throng this
area nearly every day! The café is open mainly at weekends in winter

and all week during the summer. The opening times are 10-ish to 4-ish. Give them a call if you want more information. There's a good choice of food with soup, warm Derbyshire oatcake, lasagne and hot toasted sandwiches available, as well as Derbyshire cream tea, fruit scone and spiced teacake from Hobb's Bakery. Remember, it's best to eat *after* the walk rather than before or you will never get up that hill. Telephone: 01629 640346.

DISTANCE: 3½ miles.
MAP: OS Explorer OL24 – The Peak District (White Peak Area).
STARTING POINT: Monsal Head, near Little Longstone (GR 185715).
HOW TO GET THERE: Monsal Head is on the B6465 between Ashford in the Water and Wardlow Mires. Use the large District Council car park behind the Monsal Head Hotel.

THE WALK

1. Walk to the car park entrance and turn left, then left again to reach the front of the hotel and admire the view. Walk along the road past Hobb's Café. Pass through one of the gaps in the wall ahead as the road bends sharply right downhill. Turn immediately right down the path with the road to your right. Continue down this path, ignoring all others to the left. In the valley bottom walk alongside some farm buildings, turning left immediately past the last one. Bear right over the footbridge that straddles the Wye. You will see Hobb's Café high above you.

2. Beyond the bridge, bear half-right to ascend a path. Don't cross the brick bridge over the Monsal Trail when you reach it – go through the small gate and keep forward to the trail. Bear right along this, forking left on reaching a small building. This brings you to a stony track, where you should turn left. This is a steep climb and quite hard going, ignore the bridleway on the left. The track swings right, uphill, keep on the track until you reach a second gateway. When you come out from under the trees Upperdale is visible down to your right, as well as Cressbrook Mill (with Cressbrook's houses above it), for a short while, depending on how quickly you're walking at this stage! The track levels slightly and ahead, in the trees, is Brushfield Hough, which you'll walk through in due course. Fin Cop is visible to your left across the other side of the dale and below it the messy stack of rocks known as

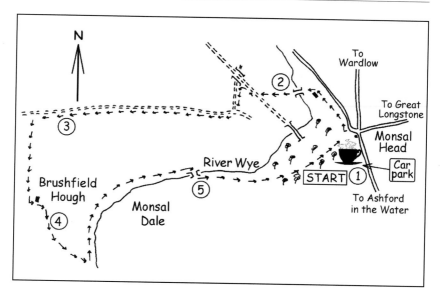

Hob's House. The track begins to swing away from the lip of the dale.

3. Pass through a gate into the fields. Climb a step-over by a second gate and walk forward for 10 yards before turning left through a gap. Head to the gateway on the opposite side of the field. Follow the stony track beyond towards Brushfield Hough. Pass through a gate and continue along the track between an old stone barn on the left and a metal barn on the right. At the end of the stone barn turn left through a gateway, walk straight forward for 20 yards or so before bearing right to a gate out of the farmyard. Thirty yards later pass through another gate and proceed along a track leading away from the farm.

4. As the track bears round to the right, cross the stile on the left. With your back to the stile, turn right into the hawthorns. The path then swings left and downhill as you enter a shady world infrequently touched by the sun. As a result the path can be a little slippery at times, so take care. At the bottom of the dale and on joining a path running from left to right, turn left to pick up the main route in the valley (with the River Wye on your right). After walking through the trees you should come out into the open and in this area do look out

47

The weir in Monsal Dale

for black rabbits – they are out there. Keep on the main path, ignoring any paths to the right. Eventually you will see a metal footbridge on the right, which please cross.

Much of Monsal Dale is owned by the Chatsworth Estate and the Wye is very popular with fishermen. Shooting also takes place occasionally in the dale so care should always be taken when walking there. Pass through at dusk (or dawn) though and you might be lucky enough to see badgers rooting around in the grass on the far side of the river.

☕ **5.** Follow the footpath nearest the river to reach the weir. Then start to ascend the narrow path through the wood. This is a fairly steep climb initially but it levels out before rising to Monsal Head.

Walk 11
BAKEWELL

You will soon leave the crowds behind as you walk up Station Road out of Bakewell and reach the Monsal Trail. Unfortunately (or perhaps fortunately) the majority of visitors to Bakewell never get far from the side of the river and the shops. This is a cracking walk whether you do it in spring, summer, autumn or winter – lovely views tinged with poignancy. Remember, the Monsal Trail was once the railway line that linked Manchester with London. This was a working landscape. Spare a thought for the men who spent their working lives here, supporting their families. After the Monsal Trail you walk through the fields back towards Bakewell and on the outskirts you descend through the wonderful scenery towards the spire of All Saints church in the valley below.

☕ It's a few years since I went into the tearoom at the Old Original Bakewell Pudding Shop. What an oversight. What an omission. Whisper it quietly but I think it is one of the best tea rooms I have ever been in. There really isn't enough space to do it justice. Pay it a visit to see what I mean. The only drawback is that it may get too busy at times, so get there early! It is open seven days a week, all year round. There is a wide, wide choice. There's the Big Bakewell Breakfast; specials such as homemade blueberry and almond tart and salmon and scrambled egg on toast. Their generous slices of cake (lemon, Victorian sponge, etc.) come with cream to one side so you can choose whether to have some or not. Then, of course, there are the Bakewell Puddings (please don't ask for a Bakewell tart). They are sweet, so be prepared. You can even 'Post A Pudding' to any part of the world. Opening times are 9 am until 5.30 pm. Closed Christmas Day. Telephone 01629 812193.

DISTANCE: 4¼ miles.

MAP: OS Explorer OL24 – the Peak District (White Peak Area).

STARTING POINT: Bakewell Agricultural Centre (GR 222685).

HOW TO GET THERE: As you enter Bakewell from the south on the A6, turn right for the Agriculture Centre. With the Agriculture Centre buildings to your right, you enter the car parking area. Note the toilets to the left by a footbridge.

THE WALK

1. From the car park return to the footbridge over the stream by the public toilets. Cross the footbridge and keep forward to cross another over the River Wye. Turn right with the river on your right. There are usually plenty of wildfowl waiting to be fed around here. On reaching the old stone bridge over the river rise up to the road and cross it carefully.

2. On the far side of the bridge, fork right along Station Road. Ignore Coombs Road to the right, continuing uphill on Station Road. It swings round to the left, still rising uphill. Some 250 yards beyond the left-hand bend, where a number of roads meet, keep forward (still on Station Road) to reach the Peak Park pay and display car park at Bakewell Station. Pass to the left of the old station building to get onto the Monsal Trail.

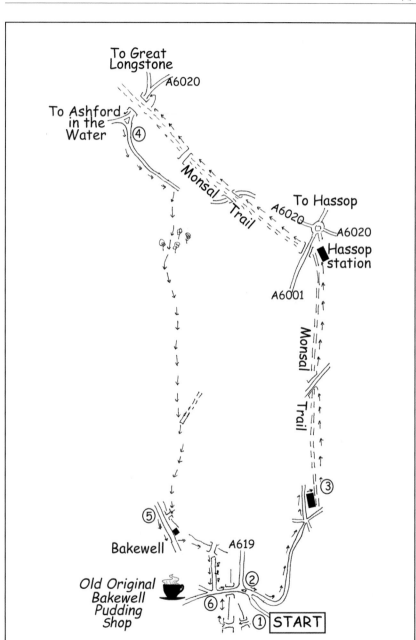

To Great
Longstone

A6020

To Ashford
in the
Water

④

Monsal Trail

To Hassop

A6020

A6020

Hassop
station

A6001

Monsal Trail

③

⑤

Bakewell

A619

Old Original
Bakewell
Pudding
Shop

②

⑥

① START

3. Turn left on the Monsal Trail to reach Hassop Station, one mile later. Stay on the Trail and pass under a bridge almost immediately beyond Hassop Station. Ignore a bridleway that crosses the Trail and which leads to Toll Bar House to the right. Keep forward. A bridge takes you over the A6020. You then pass under a bridge linking fields on either side of the Trail. Immediately before you cross a bridge over another road, turn right down to the road. Turn left under the bridge – taking great care as you do so. At the grass triangle fork left to reach the A6020 which you crossed on the Trail earlier.

4. Turn left on the A6020. After 300 yards, on the left-hand bend in the road (and with a red-brick wall across the road on your left), pass through the squeezer stile on your right. Bear half left across the field, keeping just to the left of the slope in the field. Continue in the same direction towards a small gate leading into the wood, known as Cracknowl Wood. Follow the path up through the wood. After 300 yards leave the wood via a step-over stile. In the field (with your back to the stile) head half right towards the left-hand side of the trees across the field. As you proceed, you will see a cottage to the left of the trees – aim for the 5ft-high metal kissing gate to the left of the cottage. In the field beyond the kissing gate, keep forward aiming for the far left-hand corner 500 yards away. As you go, don't pass through the field gate to your left on the brow of the rise, go through the wicket gate just beyond. Walk down the field from the wicket gate, bearing slightly left to pass a wall projecting into the field. Beyond this, keep in the same direction towards a gate in the bottom left-hand corner of the field. Cross the stile by the gate to come out onto a walled bridleway. Turn right here and cross another stile a few yards away. This brings you to a dewpond (or perhaps it's a mere). Head down the field in the general direction of Bakewell church spire over ½ mile away. Pass through a gate at the bottom of the field. Follow the track downhill from the gate passing an old quarry and some works. When you reach Holme Hall to your left at the bottom of the hill, turn right to reach a packhorse bridge. Cross this to reach the A6.

☕ **5.** Turn left along the A6. In 200 yards, having passed the fire station on your left, turn left immediately beyond Victoria Mill. Keep forward to pass through a gap immediately to the left of the entrance gate to Milford House. Follow the stream on your left to reach a quaint stone bridge. Turn right on reaching the bridge (you don't cross it). Walk along the street (which tuns out to be Castle Street) until you reach the Castle public house.

6. Cross the road here and retrace your route back to your car with the River Wye on your left this time. If, after crossing the road, you turn right towards the roundabout on the A6 you will pass the Old Original Bakewell Pudding Shop on your left. You may want to change out of any muddy footwear first, of course.

Walk 12
BASLOW

Far-reaching views and beautiful scenery abound on this, a walk full of interest. It will also provide a chance to see whether those new boots are waterproof as invariably there will be some standing water on one or two of the paths unless the weather has been particularly dry and hot. After walking northwards below Baslow Edge the return route follows a southerly route above the Edge. After descending from the moorland, a lovely under-used path leads you through the top of Yeld Wood before an optional loop at the end passes near to Chatsworth Park and a thatched cottage.

 Standing beside the green it's named after, the Café on the Green is a very popular port of call for visitors to the village of Baslow. There is a wide range of tasty meals with breakfast available to 12 noon(ish) – bacon, sausage, beans, fried egg, tomatoes and toast – or what about something lighter like scrambled eggs on toast? There is also a variety of sandwiches or panini hot sandwiches filled with cheese and tomato. There are daily specials too – leek and potato bake, as well as Derbyshire oatcakes with bacon, tomato and brie, for example. Then there are the excellent homemade cakes! It is good to see that the café endeavours to use local produce as much as possible. The tea room is open seven days a week, opening at 9.30 am and closing at 5 pm, 5.30 pm at weekends. It may close earlier in the winter though. Telephone: 01246 583000.

If the tea room is closed for any reason there are a number of pubs hereabouts.

DISTANCE: 4¼ miles.
MAP: OS Explorer OL24 – The Peak District (White Peak Area).
STARTING POINT: Baslow (GR 258721).
HOW TO GET THERE: From the roundabout where the A621 joins the A619 head into Baslow. Turn left at Goose Green just before the pelican crossing. The District Council car park is on the far side of the green behind the village hall and the toilets.

THE WALK

1. Leave the car park by the exit. Cross the pelican crossing. Bear left up Eaton Hill (ignore Eaton Place and Eaton Drive). Four hundred yards later bear right at the grass triangle up Bar Road. Ignore all roads off this as you climb uphill. After 450 yards turn left onto a footpath just before the track disappears round a right-hand bend.

2. Some fine views open out now. Follow the grassy track in the first field to a wicket gate. Stay on the obvious track in the second one, though feel free to take advantage of a well placed seat in memory of Paul and Gwen Firth. As you sit there Chatsworth is to the left, Baslow ahead and to the right is Calver, with Stoney Middleton and Eyam further up the valley. Stay on the top side of the second field. Cross a stile into the third field. Then head towards a gate in the top side of this field but don't pass through it – continue on a track to the left of it. This is soon enclosed between walls. When the walled track ends proceed alongside the wall on your left to reach the boundary of the access land. Keep forward along the path ahead through the moorland (it's a bridleway actually). A hundred yards further on, keep forward where a path cuts across the one you're on. Keep straight ahead, ignoring any other paths. You should be walking generally on the level with Baslow Edge above to the right. It should remain there until the end of this paragraph! Pass through a narrow gateway in the wall. Ignore any minor paths off the bridleway you're on, keeping forward towards Curbar Edge ahead. At one stage, as you come towards the end of Baslow Edge, ignore a minor grassy path heading straight forward. This fizzles out in a boggy area. You should stay on the main path, which keeps to the right of this marshy area before bearing left and descending slightly to reach a wall corner jutting out towards you on your left. Pass through the narrow gateway 10 yards later to leave the access land.

3. Keep forward for 50 or 60 yards, then fork right and pass through a squeezer on the top side of this area. Proceed uphill through a couple of stiles to the road. Turn right along the verge. A hundred yards before reaching the car park on the left, turn right through a gate, back onto the access land. Stay on the main path, though after 50 yards you can fork right to a viewpoint before returning to the main path. (From the viewpoint various places will be pointed out, including Sir William Hill and Kinder Scout.) Half a mile later you reach the 15ft high Eagle Stone on the left.

The Eagle Stone is very prominent and tradition has it that young Baslow lads used to have to climb this to show that they were ready for marriage. Having tried to climb it, it has to be said that there must have been many disappointed sweethearts. There is a slightly ominous side to the stone as some say it is connected with witchcraft and 'eagle' is apparently a corruption of 'eggle' or 'aigle' meaning a witch.

Continue past the stone. At a T-junction of tracks (with the Wellington Monument to the left), turn right. Continue down the main track to pass through a gate, once again leaving the access land.

4. Descend for 400 yards. Turn left where a gate on the left is set back 5 yards from the track. Walk along the right side of the long narrow woodland beyond. Continue to the end of the wall on your right where you turn right to walk along the top side of Yeld Wood for ⅓ mile. This is full of bluebells in May and further along there are some fine old beech trees rising above you. The path eventually reaches a gate, which you should pass through, ignoring a path turning sharp left immediately before the gate. Walk forward to return to Bar Road. Turn left down here to get back to the grass triangle.

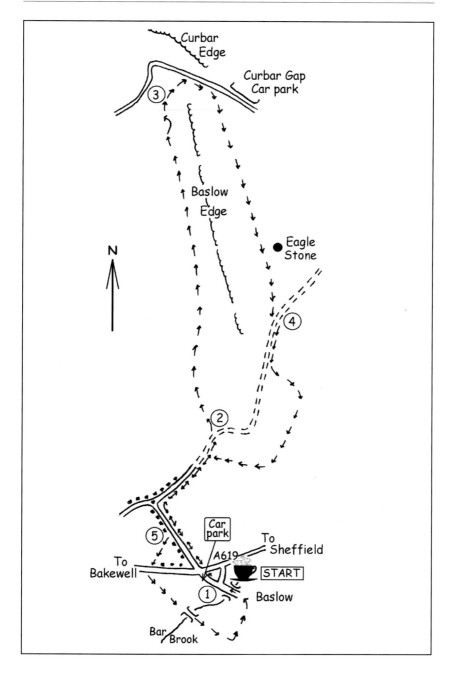

Looking across the Derwent Valley

Turn left down Eaton Hill. Continue back to the start, or if you wish to walk another ¼ mile read on!

5. Immediately beyond Ashenfell (which is immediately past Ashenbank!) turn right down the hedged path to the main road. Cross this, bearing slightly right. Descend the steps beyond the squeezer. Stay on this path as it leads to and then crosses Bar Brook. Across the other side of the field beyond the brook you reach a path leading into Chatsworth Park (to the right); you should turn left, though. Follow the track all the way back into Baslow. Just beyond the thatched cottage on the right turn left over Bar Brook again. This brings you to Goose Green with the Café on the Green on your right.

Walk 13
MONYASH

A flattish, high-level walk around this White Peak village featuring both the High Peak Trail and the Limestone Way. For good measure you'll also cross a Roman road- the A515 near the Bull i' th' Thorn pub runs almost straight for 2 miles. Monyash was a Quaker stronghold for 200 years; the old meeting-house stands just a little further along the road from the car park. It now appears to be unused, though the plain Quaker headstones still stand in the graveyard at the back. The flora around this area is particularly interesting and if you walk the route in summer, you'll see no end of colourful flowers. One thing you will notice, though, is that there aren't any woods to speak of up here. It can be a cool, uninviting place when the wind's blowing.

 Whenever the subject of tea rooms in the Peak District is raised, the Old Smithy is one that seems to get mentioned more than any others – and it's mentioned in an approving fashion! With the village green straight in front of it, it is easy to find, and with its friendly, easy going atmosphere you should enjoy it. Good wholesome food is the order of the day – soup of the day, cheese on toast, chip bap – that sort of thing. Or what about a main meal billed as 'Smithy's Breakfast – THE WORKS!'? Sounds interesting. You'll have to try it to find out what it comprises and report back. There's a vegetarian breakfast too, which is a nice idea. This comprises oatcake, cheese, egg, mushrooms, tomatoes, beans and toast. Look out for the specials too, butcher burgers and scrambled egg with cold smoked salmon being just two examples. There are, of course, cakes: carrot cake, sticky toffee gateau and chocolate fudge cake give you some idea of what's on offer. The tea rooms are open from 9 am until 6 pm at the weekend and during the rest of the week they open from 10 am until 5 pm. They will also open on special occasions if you want to book them. Telephone: 01629 810190 (or 814510, in the evening).

If you do happen to catch the tea room when it's closed, the Bull's Head is right next door. You can't miss it.

DISTANCE: 5¾ miles.
MAP: OS Explorer OL24 – The Peak District (White Peak Area).
STARTING POINT: Monyash (GR 150666).
HOW TO GET THERE: Enter Monyash along the B5055 from Bakewell. Turn right immediately beyond the Bull's Head. The small car park is along the road on the left. Roadside parking is also available thereabouts.

THE WALK

1. Take the path into the field at the back of the car park to reach September Cottage. Bear left, following the path between walls. At the back of the cottages enter the field and turn left to pass through a gap and aim for a squeezer stile ahead. This brings you to a walled track, which you should cross. Beyond this continue in a straight line until you reach Cross Lane, a walled track. In June, some of the fields around here are covered in a carpet of buttercups.

2. Turn right along the track. Ignore a track forking to the left but take the second one to the left 500 yards after joining Cross Lane. This second track, just before the stone barn, takes you along Hutmoor Butts for just over a mile – a straight, walled, track leading you to the A515 beside the Bull i' th' Thorn, one of the oldest pubs in Derbyshire. Look out for the donkeys at Newton Farm just before you reach the A515.

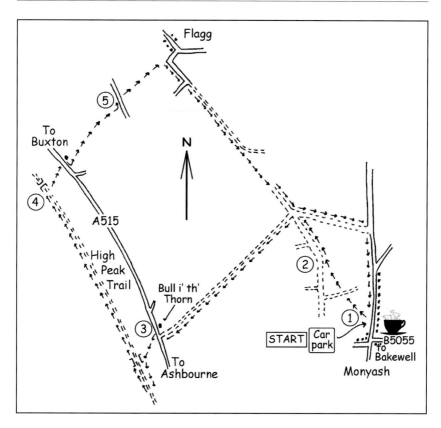

3. Turn right along the main road for 30 yards. Then cross to a stile by a gate opposite the entrance to the Bull i' th' Thorn. Walk directly away from the A515 to cross a stile, then a second one 20 yards to the right of a dewpond. In the third field after the road, bear half-left towards the buildings on the hillside. This leads to a point where the High Peak Trail is above you. Don't pass under the trail though, go through a gate to walk alongside the trail above to your right. Eventually you gain access to the trail itself, which makes use of a disused railway line. Turn sharp right here to head northwards.

As you proceed try to imagine the scene 60 or 70 years ago as trains ran up and down this line. The trail follows the route of the Cromford and High Peak Railway and runs for some 17 miles from Cromford Canal to Hurdlow – just along the trail from where you are. The railway line itself, however, used to

*run further, bypassing Buxton and heading all the way on to Whaley Bridge.
Some of it can still be followed, though beyond Hurdlow a section has been
quarried away.*

4. Nearly 1 mile later turn right over a stile immediately before the
high red (and blue) brick bridge above the trail. Walk up the slope
beyond and keep forward, bearing slightly left, to walk alongside the
wall. At the end of the field pass through a gate. Cross the yard to a
stile in front of the road. The Duke of York pub stands across the road.
Turn right for a few yards, cross the road and climb the stile into the
field beyond. Then aim for a stile beside a gate at the bottom of the
field. In the second field walk alongside a short stretch of wall on your
left, before bearing half-left towards Flagg a mile away. Keep in the
same general direction in the third field to reach the far corner (where
you pass through a pair of stiles which are close together). Walk to the
copse of trees (known as Pasture Barn, though there is no barn)
diagonally opposite. Walk through a gate and proceed through the
following field keeping to the left with the wall on your left-hand side
– ignoring a track going off to the right. You will then reach Pasture
Lane.

☕ **5.** Turn left for 75 yards. Take the stile on the right and walk
down the right side of three fields to reach a road. Turn right along
this – look out for Limestone Way signs, the route of which you will
be following all the way back to Monyash. After 250 yards, where the
road bends right, keep forward along a track ahead. Stay on this until
it bears left away from the wall towards a farm. At this point stay beside
the wall on your right to cross a stile. In the field beyond, keep straight
forward to cross another stile in the wall ahead. Then head half-right
to the far corner of the next field. Climb a stile and walk along the
walled path beyond. This brings you back to the stone outbuilding
you passed to the left of, earlier in the day. Keep on the left side of this
open area to follow a track ahead, ignoring a stile on the left as you go.
This track (Blackwell Lane) rises gently before descending to
Dalehouse Farm. Turn right at the road back into Monyash. On the
way look out for the pinfold on your right. Subsequently ignore the
road to the left. Keep forward, back to your starting point.

Walk 14
ROWSLEY

A level walk in the Peak District isn't always easy to find but here's one that runs up one side of the lovely Derwent valley before returning down the other. Starting at Rowsley you initially stroll along the Derwent Valley Heritage Way which takes you into the hamlet of Calton Lees. Crossing the River Derwent by the old stone bridge on the edge of Chatsworth Park, the path to Beeley gives great views of the woodland on your right. From the Chatsworth estate village of Beeley the varied route returns to Rowsley, where you get the chance to enjoy some tasty food at Caudwell's Country Parlour.

 Caudwell's Country Parlour is one of my favourite tea rooms and this is reflected by the number of patrons. Every time I go there I have homity pie and a full salad. I just love it. There are other tasty dishes such as courgette and tomato quiche and mushroom and hazelnut pie. As you will have gathered it is a mainly vegetarian menu. If you have any space left, then do try a generous slice of one of their homemade cakes. They open from 10 am until 5.30 pm every day except Christmas Eve, Christmas Day and Boxing Day. They usually close for a week in January, too. Telephone 01629 733185 (and ask to be put through to the Country Parlour).

DISTANCE: 4½ miles.
MAP: OS Explorer OL24 – the Peak District (White Peak Area).
STARTING POINT: Rowsley Recreation Ground (GR 256656).
HOW TO GET THERE: From the A6 in Rowsley, turn onto School Lane opposite the Peacock. The recreation ground is just beyond the bridge. Park at the roadside. Please do **not** park in the Caudwell's Mill car park whilst you go for your walk.

THE WALK

1. Return to the A6 from the recreation ground. Cross the road and walk up Church Lane, immediately to the left of the Peacock (noting the 1652 date over the door). Some 120 yards beyond the hotel, turn right on a footpath to pass under the old railway line. There should be a signpost at the roadside for Calton Lees and Chatsworth. This path forms part of the Derwent Valley Heritage Way. Beyond the bridge follow the track (which can be muddy) as it swings right. The River Derwent should be to your right. The track swings left to some extent then right with the river never very far away. The track eventually runs between some banking immediately to your left and the river immediately to your right. At the end of this short stretch of path you enter a field. Proceed alongside the trees on your left. This brings you to a wall on your left which you should follow to reach a wood. Walk through this.

2. On the far side of the wood, bear half left towards the plantation on the hillside ahead. Just over 100 yards later swing right to walk through the centre of the field. Aim for a gateway. Beyond this, in the second field, aim towards another gateway ahead and cross a stile to the side of the gate. Walk up the left side of the field beyond. Just beyond the wood on your left, climb a stile on your left and turn right so you are walking alongside a wall on your right. If you walk near to the wall (along what was once an old track), you reach a gate. Ignore this and proceed to a stile beside a second gate.

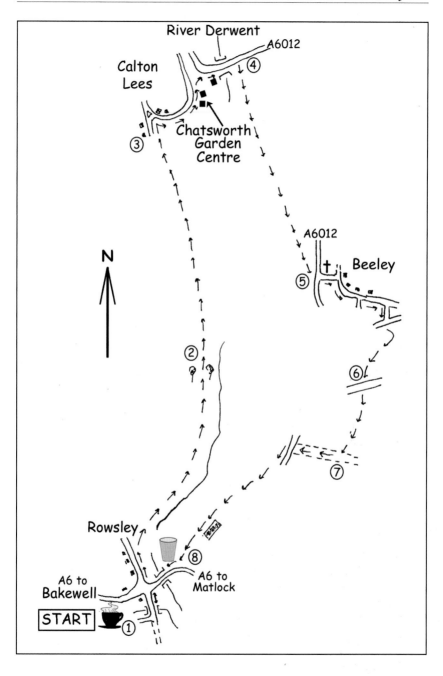

3. You are now in Calton Lees with plenty of Chatsworth 'blue' on the estate houses. Keep forward along the lane. At a grass triangle, swing right along a lane. The lane swings left taking you beside the garden centre over the wall on your right. When you reach the entrance to the garden centre, turn right and cross this. Follow a path down the banking, through the trees, to reach a road below. Turn right over the road-bridge.

4. Turn right through a kissing gate beyond the bridge and walk through the long field for ½ mile.

5. On the far side of the field cross the road carefully to enter the village of Beeley. Walk up the road with the churchyard on your left. St Anne's church dates from the late 12th century and is Beeley's oldest building. It was restored in the late 19th century. Swing right beyond the churchyard at the T-junction. At the grass triangle, fork left passing Cavendish village hall on your left. Pass Dukes Barn on your left, too. Immediately beyond Pynot Cottage bear right down a short stretch of lane. Cross the stone footbridge over Beeley Brook at the bottom and pass through the stile beyond. Rise up the slope, first bearing left and then right. Pass through a gap into another field and walk to the lane beyond.

6. Cross the lane and pass through a wicket gate. Walk on the right side of the first field and then a second. Pass through another wicket gate at the end of the second field, turning left immediately to pass through another wicket gate a few yards away. Pass through a squeezer stile just beyond that to enter a small copse. At the far side of the trees pass through another narrow gate. Walk forward to pass through yet another wicket gate. Cross the top end of a field and pass through another gate. Keep beside the hedge on your left until you reach and pass through another wicket gate beneath a large tree. Turn right immediately beyond and walk alongside the hedge and then a wall to pass through yet another gate! Ignore a couple of stone step stiles hereabouts. Walk along the bottom side of the field to reach a track.

7. Turn right down the track to reach a road 180 yards later. Turn left along the road for 400 yards. Immediately beyond Sunny Lea turn right down the path towards the River Derwent. Follow this as it descends and walk beside the river on your right. As the river veers away from the path, keep forward towards the allotments, keeping them on your right. Ignore all paths to left and right. At the end of the allotments (which double as hen pens in some cases) bear right. On reaching a double farmgate with a field beyond, turn left and follow the path between fences to come out near Peak Village. Keep forward with the buildings of Peak Village on your left and its car park to your right. Just before the last of the buildings on your left, fork right and walk through the car park of the Grouse and Claret.

8. On reaching the A6, turn right, cross the river and then fork left along School Lane back to your car and the Caudwell Country Parlour.

Walk 15
UPPER HULME

If you're very, very lucky you may see the feral wallabies on this walk around The Roaches. It's very, very unlikely but ... who knows? They are apparently still there, having been sighted recently after not having been seen for a couple of years or so. It seems they escaped some years ago from a private zoo nearby. Keep your eyes peeled. As regards The Roaches, they get their name from the French word for rock, namely 'roche'. There can be few more unusual outcrops of rock anywhere in England. It is very much a unique landscape in this crowded island of ours. As you drive to the start of the walk and see the view unfold before you, you will get some idea of the enjoyable walk you'll have.

The Roaches Tea Rooms now fully licensed (shown as Paddock Farm on the OS White Peak Map) is gloriously positioned at the foot of The Roaches from where there are lovely views across the valley in front. The tea rooms are open every day of the year except from Christmas Eve to Boxing Day (inclusive). From March to October the opening times are from 9 am to 5 pm, closing one hour earlier (4 pm) November to February. What about the food? Well, the cakes and puddings are all homemade and there are tasty specials such as Staffordshire oatcakes, along with various light meals, sandwiches, omelettes, baked potatoes and paninis. Being a tea room you will be pleased that a 'cream tea' (or coffee) is available – this comprises a scone with jam, cream and a pot of tea or coffee. If you're visiting on a hot summer's day, sit outside and be prepared to bake – it's a real sun-trap. Telephone: 01538 300345.

If you've enjoyed your visit to the area you can even stay on as there are two holiday cottages at Paddock Farm. If the tea room is closed then there is a pub in Upper Hulme ½ mile or so away, where you may be able to recharge your batteries.

DISTANCE: 5¼ miles.

MAP: OS Explorer OL24 – The Peak District (White Peak Area).

STARTING POINT: The Roaches, near Upper Hulme (GR 007613).

HOW TO GET THERE: Travelling north on the A53 from Leek, about 3 miles from Leek town centre, turn left at the Upper Hulme signpost. Keep left (ignoring all right turns) and ¾ mile later you reach The Roaches tea room. Park on the road opposite or further along to cut down on road-walking! The route is described from the tea room. Please do not park in the Roaches Tea Rooms car park before you go for a walk.

THE WALK

1. From the teashop walk along the road away from Upper Hulme. Pass the driveways to Roaches Hall (on the right) and to Windygates Hall Farm (on the left). Three hundred yards later, beyond a left-hand bend, take the footpath on your right (to the left of a small door in the wall!). This brings you onto the Roaches Estate, owned by the Peak National Park. Ascend the right side of the field. Where the path levels out, with a wicket gate on your right, turn left and cross the field to another wicket gate. Immediately beyond this turn right along a track beside the wall on your right. Pass by another wicket gate, the track now moving away from the wall. Continue until you pass a single stone gate post. From here descend gently, still on the same path. The view changes with scattered farmsteads ahead of you. The path, though, bears left away from these farms.

2. Pass through a gate on your right to maintain direction, following

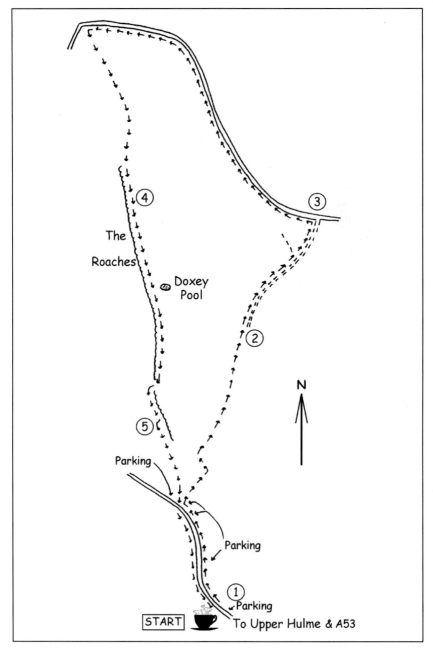

Looking along the Roaches towards Hen Cloud in the distance

the track between fences beyond. Subsequently cross a stile to leave the Roaches Estate. Keep forward on the track to reach a lane.

3. Turn left on the lane and steadily rise up. You will be on this lane for 1½ miles but the views are splendid and it's fairly quiet too.

For the last ½ mile or so, you'll notice some 4 miles ahead of you the unmistakable outline of Shutlingsloe (over 1,600ft above sea level).

Eventually the lane gradually descends. Where it takes a sharp turn to the left (with a bridleway to the right and a squeezer stile ahead of you) turn sharp left up a paved path with steps to ascend to a wall on the right with a pair of boulders beyond. Keep beside the wall for 40 yards until it bears away from the path. The path is then surfaced with flagstones and an excellent view of Tittesworth Reservoir can be enjoyed. And that's the Wrekin far away to your right. Continue until the flagstones end and you're following a sandy path.

4. At the trig point there are fine views all around. Continue beyond this, keeping as near to the high ground as possible to reach Doxey Pool ¾ mile later.

It's quite a surprise to find a small pool here, so high up. Some say it never dries up and there are others who say there's a mermaid waiting to lure unsuspecting passers-by to a watery death. You've been warned so take care!

Stay on the high ground. A quarter of a mile beyond the pool leave the ridge path to turn right down a gully. Ignore a left fork almost as soon as you've walked through the narrowest section of this 'gully' and continue forward until, 50 yards later, you turn left along a level path beneath the conifers. The path brings you to a huge rock outcrop which seems to have been forced into the ground at an angle. Turn right to take the long flight of steps descending the near side of the rock.

☕ **5.** At the bottom of the steps continue forward for 60 yards to pass through a gap in the bottom wall. Turn left and follow the stony footpath. On your left at this point is Rockhall Cottage, the Don Whillans Memorial Hut – Don Whillans being a famous climber.

Look out for the 15ft-high boulder (with steps cut in it) standing beside Rockhall sub-station!

Keep forward across a track and pass through a wicket gate ahead. Walk across the field to the stile in the bottom corner of the field that you passed through near the start of the walk. Return to your car – wherever it's parked.

Walk 16
HARTINGTON

This walk was devised on a summer's evening with a thunderstorm rolling ahead of us as we walked along the lane with Sheen to our left. Whilst that memory may fade it is unlikely to die. With luck the elements will spare you the spectacle of a heavy and noisy storm and you can relax and enjoy this quieter part of the countryside surrounding Hartington. Whilst Dovedale, to the south of the village, is often heaving with walkers, this area, to the north, sees fewer visitors. If you get the chance to walk this on a balmy summer evening or a sunny warm day, try to have a stop as you cross the Dove near Pilsbury. In summer the swallows swoop low across the river to scoop up a drink of water, and there's something therapeutic about the sound of running water.

It's good to know that some English villages still have a pub and a post office. Hartington has quite a bit more, to be honest, including a cheese shop – try to pay it a visit. Don't forget to visit the Beresford Tea Rooms too. There is a wide range of appetising food, with something for everyone. Whether you fancy tucking into a cheese and onion toastie or a jacket potato with baked beans and salad or perhaps an All Day Breakfast, then you should come out of the tea rooms feeling satisfied. You could try one of the specials, too – Derbyshire filled oatcakes or homemade hotpot with a baguette, perhaps? The Beresford Tea Rooms are open every day from 9 am until 5 pm in summer and, in winter, from 10 am until 4 pm during the week and from 10 am until 4.30 pm at the weekend. Telephone: 01298 84418.

There are other tea rooms and pubs in Hartington if the Beresford Tea Rooms are closed or busy.

DISTANCE: 5¾ miles.
MAP: OS Explorer OL24 – The Peak District (White Peak Area).
STARTING POINT: Hartington (GR 128604).
HOW TO GET THERE: If you enter Hartington from the north-east, along the B5054, proceed through the village and use the District Council car park on the right just as you leave the village.

THE WALK
Note: The walk down the track at the beginning of point 3 can be a bit of a scramble in one short section.

1. Turn left out of the car park and walk along the road. Find the Corner House near the village pond and walk down Stonewell Lane to the right of it (as you look at it). Turn right through the wicket gate at the entrance to the cheese factory.

The cheese factory has now closed. It used to be one of the few places in the country that made Stilton cheese. The Old Cheese Shop is still open thankfully.

Bear left through the trees at the end of the first field. In the second field head towards the plantation on the hillside ahead. Cross the corner of the third field. Walk diagonally across the fourth field. Bear slightly left to a gateway in the hedge in the fifth field. Bear right to a bridge over the Dove.

2. Beyond this (in Staffordshire) walk directly up the field to the large tree by the gate. Turn right onto the track. Some 75 yards further on, fork left up the green grassy path leading to the plantation you were heading towards earlier. Walk through the top side of the plantation and along the top of the bank beyond. After climbing a stone step-over, with an open field ahead, proceed slightly right and subsequently climb another step-over. Through the next four fields walk along the right side of a wall with the distinctive rocky outcrop of Sheen Hill slightly left of you. Pass through a stile to the left of the buildings of a farm, keeping left to pass through a stile by the entrance gate to the farm. Turn right and continue along the lane for ½ mile.

3. Just before the left turn to Brund turn right down the old track which takes you back into the valley of the River Dove. On your left, towards the valley bottom, is Broadmeadow Hall. As mentioned earlier, if you get the chance to stop awhile in the valley bottom it will be worth it. Rise up the track beyond the river to the lane at Pilsbury. [At this point there is an option open to you. If the weather is unpleasant or you don't fancy a climb up into the fields above Pilsbury, you can turn right along the quiet, gated lane for a couple of miles to get back into Hartington.] If you're going to do the full walk then turn left along the lane and zigzag up the hillside behind the houses. It's a steepish climb but worth it for the views.

Although you won't be able to see it there's a Norman motte and bailey away to your left. Presumably Pilsbury was rather busier 1,000 years ago than it is now. Today, there is little to see on the ground other than some earthworks.

Immediately before a newish building made of corrugated sheets, turn right over a stile. Bear half-left for 40 yards to pass by a single gate post. Head through the shallow valley ahead for 400 yards.

4. On reaching a stile turn right without crossing it! Climb up the steep bank to another stile. Cross this. Walk to the far end of the wall ahead on your left. You'll see it is, in fact, a wall corner when you reach it. Continue in the same direction to reach a second wall corner. Bear left here to reach a farm gate 130 yards further on. Pass through the small gate beside it. Proceed to the gap in the wall across the other side of the field. Bear half-right to pass through a stile in the bottom left-hand corner of the field. Keep forward for 15 yards before bearing slightly left through a low 'nick' in the rocks. Now keep straight forward, aiming for the left-hand side of a number of hills on the horizon – below these are the buildings of Bank Top Farm. You should be aiming just to the left of them. Climb one stile, then a

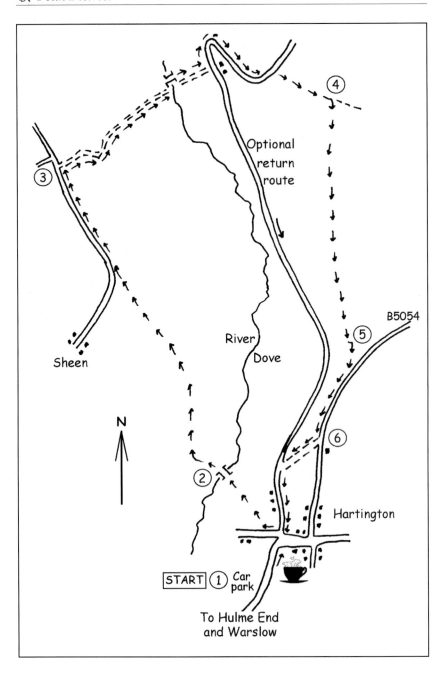

second. Pass through a 'gateway' (with that hill beyond!), walking beside a tumbled-down wall on the left for 50 or 60 yards. There are no distinguishing features (except some waymark posts at the time of writing) for some distance – but you should still be heading for the left-hand hill. Keep to the left of a 15-yard length of dilapidated wall facing you, then bear ever so slightly left to reach a wall corner 150 yards ahead. Keep to the right of this to walk along a 'shelf of ground with Bank Top Farm down to the right. You should reach a gate with a concrete track beyond.

5. Turn left, up this track. Go through the wicket gate just beyond a five-bar gate across the track. Turn right and continue for 60 yards to climb a step-over stile. Then head for the gable end of the outbuilding made of corrugated sheeting. Turn half-left in the next field and slightly right in the one after that, towards the far end of the outbuilding, to reach the lane.

☕ **6.** Turn right down the lane for 250 yards, where, just before the house on the left, fork right down a grassy lane to reach a lower (tarmac) lane. Turn left here back into Hartington.

Walk 17
CROMFORD

Though this walks starts just outside the Peak District, it stands comparison with all the other routes in this book. In the first half you get to walk in the footsteps of Alison Uttley, who wrote A Traveller in Time *as well as the* Little Grey Rabbit *and* Sam Pig. *As you stroll through Bow Wood, think of the young schoolgirl at the end of the 19th century walking through here on her way to school in Lea. We wouldn't let our children do that nowadays, would we ...? The second stretch of the walk sees you alongside Cromford Canal, a lovely (and popular) canal, where you must look out for the little grebe (or dabchick) as it ducks underwater as soon as you look at it. I've seen a 2-foot pike in the water near the car park so look out for that, too.*

Recently opened by the Arkwright Society (a charity active in preserving local industrial monuments), Wheatcroft's Wharf is in a great position beside the start (or is it the finish?) of the Cromford canal. As well as being a tea room, it's also a shop so have a browse around when you're there. The food is largely homemade, including items such as oven-baked jacket potatoes, soup (such as mushroom and celery), paninis (cheese and ham or brie and tomato) and filled rolls with fillings, including cheese and tomato chutney. There are specials too, for instance, homemade meatloaf served with salad and cheese and onion quiche with a large mixed salad. It's well worth a visit. Wheatcroft's Wharf opens from 9 am until 4.45 pm in winter and from 10 am until 5.45 pm in summer. Telephone: 01629 823256 (and ask for Wheatcroft's Wharf).

DISTANCE: 3½ miles.
MAP: OS Explorer OL24 – the Peak District (White Peak Area).
STARTING POINT: Cromford Wharf car park (GR 299570).
HOW TO GET THERE: From the A6 in Cromford, follow Mill Lane. Follow this road
    until you reach Cromford Wharf which is the second car park on the right.

THE WALK

1. From the car park return to the road and turn right. Pass St Mary's church on your left. Cross the bridge over the river carefully and swing round to the right, ignoring Willersley Lane leading up to Starkholmes on your left. Follow the level road with the River Derwent on your right. Cross the entrance to Cromford railway station and pass under the railway bridge.

2. After 40 yards take the path on the left. Stay on this as it rises uphill through the trees and shrubs. Eventually you reach a stone squeezer stile on your right leading into a wood. Turn right through this, leaving the path that continues to rise uphill through the field. Walk through the wood. At the far side, climb a step-over stile into a field. Keep forward along a 'shelf' across the bank ahead. When the 'shelf' splits, bear right downhill alongside a line of hawthorns on your right. On reaching the end of a wall on your left after 60 yards, bear half left beyond the wall to follow another 'shelf' which leads to a water trough after another 60 yards. Continue beyond this to climb another step-over stile beside a farmgate. Then aim half right to another gate. Pass through a stile onto a lane.

3. Turn left up the lane. Ignore a squeezer stile by a gate on your right

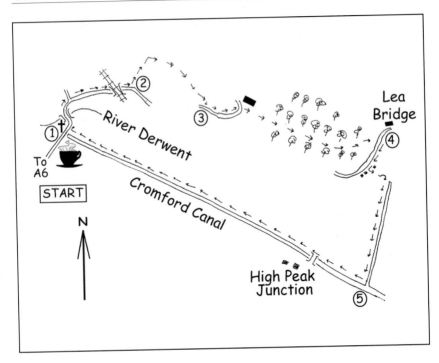

for Bow Wood Cottages. Continue to rise uphill and steadily round to the left. Where the lane swings left quite tightly (and with the entrance to Sunnybank in front of you) take the footpath below Sunnybank itself. This leads into Bow Wood which Alison Uttley used to walk through on her way to school. The path is as wide as a track initially through the wood. Keep forward ignoring a subsequent path forking left uphill. The path you're on loses a little height. Part of the wood is owned by the Woodland Trust – look out for their signs. Ignore another path forking uphill to the left. Proceed until you come out into the open with the High Peak Junction car park to your right below. Towards the end of the wood the path descends more steeply to bring you to a road.

4. Turn right here taking care as you do. Walk along the pavement beside the road towards a group of houses. Immediately past Lea Wood Cottage turn left along a driveway and then, 30 yards later, turn left again alongside the stream on your left. Then bear right to follow a walled path that brings you to a track. Turn right along the track with an arm of the canal on your left. Follow this crossing the railway line, all the way to the Cromford Canal.

5. Turn right on reaching the canal and, with the canal on your left, walk the 1¼ miles back to the start. As you go, you will pass the tall chimney of Leawood Pumphouse and, later, the buildings, (including toilets), at High Peak Junction.

Walk 18
WEAG'S BRIDGE

*B*y *the time you've driven down to Weag's Bridge you'll have experienced a foretaste of what's to come – spectacular Staffordshire scenery. This is a walk to be enjoyed at any time of the year though if there's ice on the roads you'd be best parking at Grindon! As regards the walk itself, after heading north on the Manifold Way, one of the first sights you'll see is Thor's Cave high above you. Then you reach Wetton Mill Tea Rooms, where you can have a break. It's all so green and lush around these parts. There has to be a climb at some stage in the Peak District and this one takes you up to Grindon, a pleasant village with a pub, a church, a pond and an overall feeling of peace and quiet. Then a descent along a quiet country lane (with excellent views) before a field path brings you back to the car. But who was Weag?*

Wetton Mill Tea Rooms is another tea room in a lovely setting. You may want to take a little time over your stop here, beside the River Manifold. If the weather's fine why not sit outside and enjoy the lovely scenery? There may not be a wide choice of food here but the surroundings more than make up for it. You can choose from sandwiches such as cheese and onion, cheese and pickle, ham salad, ham and pickle or tuna mayonnaise. Or what about one of the delicious cakes – sponge, chocolate or lemon? You can also get drinks and ice-creams. They're open all day from 1st April to the end of October, and open Saturday and Sunday all year. During the day they're fairly flexible and will open up at 9(ish) am and close at 5(ish) pm. Telephone: 01298 84838.

If they're closed try Ye Olde Royal Oak in Wetton.

DISTANCE: 4¾ miles.
MAP: OS Explorer OL24 – The Peak District (White Peak Area).
STARTING POINT: Weag's Bridge, near Grindon (GR 100542).
HOW TO GET THERE: From Ye Olde Royal Oak in Wetton drive downhill. Take the first right for Grindon. Pass the small car park and toilets. Ignore the right turn beyond. Continue along the lane to reach a T-junction and turn right. Proceed down the steep lane to cross the 'weak bridge' in the valley bottom. Turn right to the parking area.

THE WALK

1. With the road bridge behind you head north on the Manifold Way.

This tarmac trail in the valley was formerly the route of the Leek and Manifold Light Railway. It ran for 30 years at the beginning of the 20th century from Leek up to Waterhouses. It seems a pity in some ways that some of these lines closed down. Think what a spectacular ride you could have through this scenery.

Initially you're in the open but you soon pass under trees with the river over the wall on your right – assuming it's still running; it dries up in dry weather. You reach Ladyside Wood on your left and on your right is an interpretation panel with Thor's Cave above. By all means go and have a closer look at the cave. Our walk continues on the old railway line though. After a while you reach a lane via a bridge with railway sleepers for a base.

2. Cross the lane and enter the small parking area opposite. Pass through the stile on the far side of this (near the National Trust 'Wetton Hills' sign). Follow the grassy track up the left side of the field for ¼ mile until it swings right. Take the path (it's a bridleway actually) running sharp left at this point. Follow this as it rises up to a small

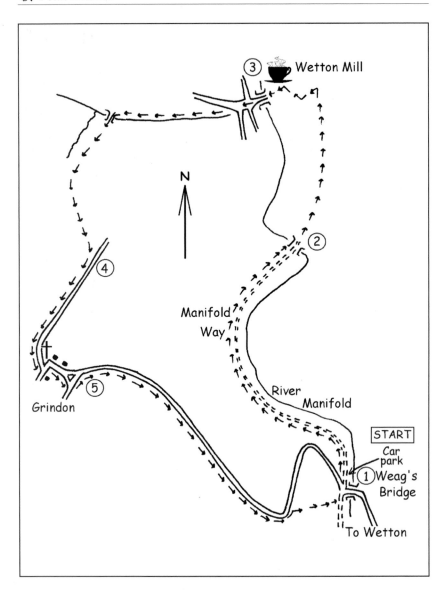

gate. Walk forward for 40 yards beyond, then turn right through a squeezer down a stony path. After 50 yards or so, bear left downhill to reach Wetton Mill and the café.

Thor's Cave above the Manifold Way

3. After your stop, cross the road bridge over the river. Keep forward to cross the road running from left to right. Follow the signpost for Butterton and, with a ford on your left, swing round to the right. Leave the road almost immediately to follow the bridleway through a bridle-gate (ignoring the footpath and footbridge to the left). Continue up the valley on the bridleway, keeping the brook on your left. This is a peaceful part of the walk with (usually) just the sound of the running water beside you. Nearly ¾ mile later cross a small (sometimes, slippery) footbridge. Ignore the stile on your right – follow the bridleway ahead for Grindon and Hillsdale. After 25 yards cross a more substantial bridge (at the bottom of Ossoms Hill). Ignoring a third footbridge almost immediately (which leads to the right) follow the bridleway for Grindon which bends gently left and upwards with a smaller stream to your right. The bridleway moves away from the stream. Pass through a bridle-gate beneath some trees. As the bridleway becomes a little steeper you'll find you have a hedgerow on your right. Stay on the right side of the next field and go through a bridlegate, following a shallow holloway in the following two fields, which will take you to a lane – you should be heading to the left of Grindon church ahead.

4. Turn right along the lane, walking into Grindon to the church. At a T-junction with the church to your left, turn left (passing the Kindle Stone on the green – a 'rindle' is a wet-weather stream).

If you visit the church you will find inside some small remains of the Handley Page Halifax Bomber that crashed on Grindon Moor on 13th February 1947, whilst bringing supplies to the villagers who had been trapped by the terrible snowfall. Six crew were lost and two press photographers. Just inside the church doorway are newspaper cuttings about this incident.

If you don't visit the church, bear right at the Old Rectory, passing it on your left. Stay on the lane until it forks, taking the right fork and then turning left at the T-junction. Continue forward to walk out of Grindon towards the east.

5. There is a footpath (in the fields) running parallel to the lane but the views from the lane are better. As you continue down the lane an impressive whaleback hill dominates the view ahead. There is a seat on the left set back from the road giving you a chance to appreciate the scenery. Continue to the sharp left-hand bend in the road and follow it round for no more than 10 yards. Then pass through the stile on the right and another on the left a few yards later. Walk down the right side of the field beyond. In the second field aim initially for the bottom left corner but in the middle of the field the path bears slightly right. Proceed onto the road and turn left back to your car.

Walk 19
TISSINGTON

Walking on trails doesn't appeal to everyone but, since the Tissington Trail opened in the early 1970s, many new circuits have opened up for walkers wanting to expore the lovely countryside around the White Peak village of Tissington. Soon after you get onto the Trail you will have a wide view of the lovely valley between Tissington and Parwich, with the tree-capped hill of Minninglow in the distance. It's easy to become blasé about the Peak District and take the landscape for granted. This is a walk that gives you the chance to really appreciate what we have.

 There can't be many villages more attractive than Tissington. Indeed, walking up the main street on a sunny day must be one of the most delightful ways to enjoy not just Derbyshire but life itself. After passing the church on your right and Herbert's Fine English Tearooms (formerly The Old Coach House) on your left, you then reach Tissington Hall in all its glory. The delights continue as you enter the lovely old building that houses the tea room. And they won't stop when you see the dishes available – homemade soup such as carrot and coriander and cream of mushroom, homemade puddings (sticky toffee pudding and hot choc fudge cake anyone?). There are different fillings for baps served with salad or you could choose some of the delicious cakes. If you like the teashop you can book it for your own private party. It's open in winter from 11 am until 5 pm (on Thursday, Friday, Saturday and Sunday) closed Christmas Day, and in the summer every day from 11 am until 5 pm. Telephone: 01335 350501.

If they're closed, head back to the main road and turn left to the Bluebell pub.

DISTANCE: 2¾ miles.
MAP: OS Explorer OL24 – The Peak District (White Peak Area).
STARTING POINT: Tissington (GR 178521).
HOW TO GET THERE: Enter Tissington from the A515. Ignore the left turn rising up towards Tissington Hall, pass the village pond on the right and continue until you can turn right into the car park on the Tissington Trail.

THE WALK

🍵 **1.** Leave the car park by the entrance and turn left towards the village of Tissington. Ignore all right turns to pass the village pond on your left. Twenty yards beyond the pond bear right up the road passing between Herbert's Fine English Tearooms on the left and St Mary's church on your right A little further on is Tissington Hall on your left and the unusually-shaped Hall Well on your right.

Tissington is well known for its welldressings and Hall Well is one of a handful of wells that are 'dressed' every year. According to one of the information panels in the village, Tissington has over 50,000 visitors during the week the wells are dressed. On Ascension Day the wells are blessed and the dressings removed a week later

The Tissington Estate has been in the hands of the FitzHerbert family since the reign of Queen Elizabeth I. The hall was built in 1609 and has been lived in by the same family ever since.

Continue up the road, ignoring the right fork to Sawpit Hill. Keep

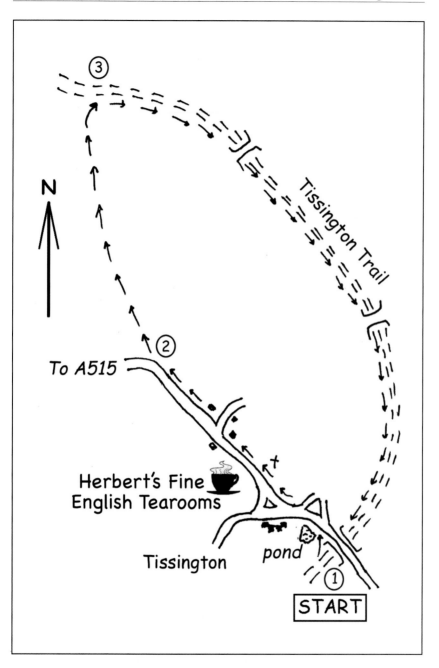

Along the way

straight ahead, climbing gradually. You leave the houses of the village behind.

2. At the left-hand bend where The Street becomes Rakes Lane, leave the tarmac behind to follow the walled path straight ahead of you. Ignore a footpath into the field on your left. At the end of the walled track, walk up the left side of the field ahead. As you walk up this field you get some idea of the medieval 'ridge and furrow' features to your right. In the first field, walking beside the wall on your left, you pass between the wall and a small copse in the field. At the end of the first field, cross a step-over stile and walk up the left side of the second field. At the end of the second field continue along a second stretch of walled path. At the end of this, keep forward, still with a wall on your left. Then you walk along a third stretch of walled path. At the end of this, bear slightly right towards a gate which will come into view as you go. Cross the stile beside the gate to reach the Tissington Trail.

3. Turn right along the Trail to follow it all the way back to the car park over a mile later.

Tissington Station was opened in August 1899 but there is little of it left. The line closed in 1963 but the Peak Park later turned it into the Tissington Trail.

Walk 20
ILAM

Ilam Hall (Ilam is pronounced Eye-lam) stands in a loop of the River Manifold, or at least it does some of the time. As you may discover, the Manifold is one of those limestone rivers that disappear in dry weather. The village is a delightful collection of quaint cottages in an idyllic setting surrounded by majestic scenery. If you've travelled into Ilam from Thorpe in Derbyshire then you'll have seen that marvellous view from the hill overlooking Ilam and probably gasped in wonder; try it in autumn and it's even more spectacular. St Bertram crops up a couple of times on this walk as you pass first his well and then a bridge named after him. Finally, mention must be made of Castern Hall in its magnificent position overlooking the Manifold valley.

☕ Just before you enter the National Trust Manifold Tea Room at Ilam Hall, look to your right – what a view: Ilam church with the flat top of Thorpe Cloud beyond. Once you enter, expect something a bit special too. There are some interesting dishes to be had and anyone who hasn't had a Staffordshire oatcake ought to try one. They're served with various fillings and hopefully Manifold toppers will still be available when you visit. The Manifold Tea Room is aiming to start a seasonal menu with deli specials making use of locally sourced meat. Bowls of seasonal soup should be on the menu too. For those who are not watching the calories (or at least not too closely) a cream tea served with jam and cream (plus a pot of tea) is also yours for the asking. Telephone: 01335 350245.

If the Manifold Tea Room is closed, head back towards Thorpe where there are a couple of pubs/hotels.

DISTANCE: 4¼ miles.
MAP: OS Explorer OL24 – The Peak District (White Peak Area).
STARTING POINT: Ilam Hall, Ilam (GR 131507).
HOW TO GET THERE: Ilam is 4½ miles north-west of Ashbourne. Park in the National Trust car park at Ilam Hall. National Trust members can park free. Alternatively, park on the roadside in the vicinity of Ilam Cross.

THE WALK

1. From the National Trust car park, walk past the 'pepper pot' at the entrance. Then proceed down the left side of the church on the gravel path to reach a tarmac access road. Turn left along this to reach the village of Ilam. Bear right and walk towards the cross near the roadbridge.

2. Fork left along the road at the cross. Immediately beyond Town End, with the Manifold on your right, take the path on the left. Ascend the path to reach a track. Turn left. After 20 yards fork right uphill for Stanshope. Pass a pond to the left that is popular with fishermen. Continue along the track to a farm gate. Here, on National Trust access land, proceed beside the wall on your left. Above you Bunster Hill rises some 329 metres above sea level (that's nearly 1,100 ft). You pass St Bertram's Well on the right. Four hundred yards beyond the gate pass a stile on the left. Continue beside the wall for another 150 yards on steeper ground. Pass through a wicket gate. Walk forward on the path ahead, keeping to the right of the trees. Where the path becomes indistinct continue to the end of the field and pass through a stile. With your back to this, walk just under half-right across the field ahead, keeping to the right of the trees in front. Do not get too far from them! Ahead, in front of a low hill, is Beechenhill Farm, which

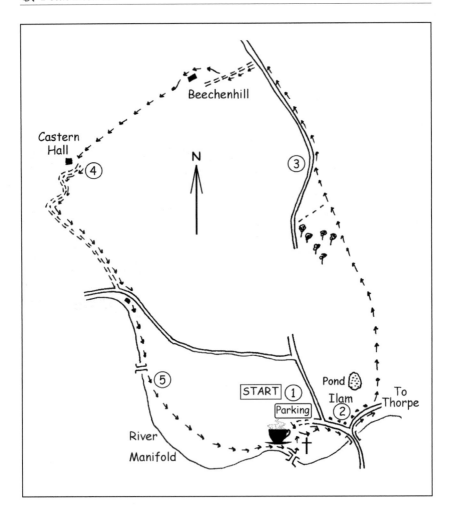

you will shortly be walking behind. Proceed forward, keeping the end of the trees some 40 or 50 yards to your left – do *not* walk downhill to cross the stile by the gate at the end of the trees! Rising gently, pass to the right of a small disused quarry, aiming for a step-over stile to the left of a gateway. Beyond this aim for another step-over to the right of the next gateway. Climb onto the lane beyond.

3. Turn right and continue for 350 yards. Turn left down the drive to Beechenhill Farm. It's now downhill all the way! Eighty yards along

The grounds of Ilam Hall

the drive pass through the wicket gate on the right. Beyond the gate, bear left behind the farmhouse until, in the corner of the field, you pass through a stile behind the farmhouse. Walk along the line of trees (planted for the many guests who have stayed at the farm). At the end of the trees, pass through the wicket gate and bear half-left to a squeezer in the wall. As you walk towards this, look out on the opposite side of the valley for the old field systems which may be visible. Beyond the squeezer bear half-right towards Castern Hall. You may be able to see the ruins of Throwley Hall across the valley. Pass through the gate in the bottom corner of the field to reach Castern Hall.

4. Bear left along the access road. Just round the corner is a fine view of the Hall itself. Stay on the tarmac driveway to reach a grass triangle in the road. As you go, ignore a path signed to the right and be thankful that this is an anti-clockwise walk; if it were not, you would have a very steep hill to climb! At the grass triangle keep forward to River Lodge. Turn right 10 yards past the house. A tablet above the window will tell you who laid the first stone when the property was built. Stay on the obvious path beside the Manifold (assuming it is running) and enter Ilam Country Park. Stay on the path. Pass a narrow footbridge on the right.

5. Ignore a track forking left uphill. Keep on the obvious path with the river on the other side of the field to your right. You reach the Battle Stone, an ancient cross shaft, on the left. Continue on the main path. Where the Manifold runs immediately beside you look out for water bubbling up from the boil holes into the river. Stay beside the river (across the grass) to reach St Bertram's Bridge, restored in 1839.

St Bertram (or Bertelin) became a hermit after his wife and child were killed by wolves. He fled to these parts and took to a life of prayer. His tomb is in the church at Ilam and many people visited it as an act of pilgrimage.

Turn left here back to the church and the start of your walk.